THE
REMINGTON
HISTORICAL TREASURY
OF AMERICAN
GUNS

THE REMINGTON HISTORICAL TREASURY OF AMERICAN GUNS

BY HAROLD L. PETERSON

A Benjamin Company/Rutledge Book

Fred R. Sammis | *Editorial Director*
Doris Townsend | *Editor*
Harry Brocke | *Art Director*
John Stevenson | *Associate Art Director*
John Sammis | *Associate Editor*
Marilyn Weber | *Production Manager*

Copyright © 1966
by Specialized Publishing Co.
Prepared and produced
by Rutledge Books, Inc.
All rights reserved under
International and Pan-American Convention
Published by The Benjamin Company
485 Madison Avenue, New York, New York 1002
Simultaneously published in Canada
Library of Congress
Catalog Card Number 66-13822
Printed in the United States of America
Second Printing 1970
SBN 87502-010-0

CONTENTS

The publishers wish to thank S. M. Alvis, Curator
of the Ilion Museum, and W. R. Googin and Associates of the Remington
Research Photographic Laboratory, for their help in producing
the illustrations for this book.

*W. R. Googin—pages 2-3, 4, 6, 12, 23, 24, 25, 26, 28 right, 29, 35 left,
41 top, 42, 46, 51, 54, 62, 67, 74, 86, 88, 113, 114, 124, 128, 131, 132, 146,
153, 155, 158-159. Ilion Museum—pages 8, 10, 15, 17 bottom, 18-19, 20,
22, 34, 36, 37, 38 left, 41 bottom, 47 right, 48, 49 top,
49 middle, 52, 53, 57, 58, 60 top, 61, 66, 68, 69, 84, 85 right, 87 top, 94,
95, 117, 120, 127, 129 right, 136, 141 bottom, 150, 151 bottom. Library of Congress—
pages 21, 50, 73, 96, 122, 123 right. Walter Vecchio—pages 30, 35 right, 60 left,
60 middle, 135, 151 top, 153, 154. Bridgeport Archives—pages 140, 141 top, 149.
The Metropolitan Museum of Art—page 28 left. The Andrew F. Lustyik Collection—
page 33. Culver—pages 17 top, 49 right, 81, 82-83, 85 top, 123 left. Bettman
Archive—pages 118, 123 bottom. National Archives (Brady Collection)—
pages 38 right, 72. National Archives (Signal Corps)—pages 137, 138-139, 142, 143.
New York Public Library Picture Collection—pages 16, 27, 39, 45, 47 left,
59, 70, 77, 79, 87 bottom, 91, 93, 119. Harper's Weekly—page 40. Century
Magazine—page 65. Du Pont "Better Living" Magazine—page 129 left.
American Heritage—pages 78, 144.
Farmer's Museum, Cooperstown, N. Y., location for photo and prop on page 146*

COLOR SECTION
*Ilion Museum—pages 98 bottom left and right, 100. Walter Vecchio—pages 97,
101, 102-103, 104, 107 top, 109 middle right, 111 bottom. Thomas Samworth—
pages 98-99 top. The Brooklyn Museum—page 105. Anne S. K. Brown Collection,
Providence, R. I.—page 106. Gilcrease Museum—page 107 bottom. West Point
Museum, Harold Von Schmidt—page 108. New York Historical Society—
page 109 top. W. R. Googin—pages 109 middle, left and bottom, 110. The
Smithsonian Institution—page 111 top. The Garst Museum—page 112 bottom.
Museum of the City of New York—page 112 top*

THE
REMINGTON
HISTORICAL TREASURY
OF AMERICAN
GUNS

INTRODUCTION

A century and a half have passed since Eliphalet Remington
made his first rifle. In that time, millions of other firearms
bearing the Remington mark have appeared. The name
has become known throughout the world. It is respected by
every hunter, every marksman and every gun collector in America,
and thousands of people who have never fired a gun
still recognize the name Remington as a standard of quality.
A reputation such as this is created only by a long series
of fine products, by a tradition of excellence. Throughout its history,
Remington has produced a large collection of outstanding firearms.
Some have been revolutionary new arms; others have
been highly refined examples of types already well-known.
All have offered the finest possible design, materials and
workmanship. Here is a treasury of some of the most important
Remington guns, and the story behind them.

CHAPTER ONE

SKILLFUL HANDS

Remington was a fine shot—no
question—but could he forge a truer
rifle than had ever been made?

SKILLFUL HANDS

"Lite" Remington knew he could make a rifle. What was more, he was sure that he could make one just as good, and possibly better than any he could buy from a dealer in his part of central New York state. After all, he was nearly twenty-three years old, and he was good with tools. He had learned to forge iron in the blacksmith shop his father, the elder Eliphalet Remington, had built to serve his own needs and those of his neighbors at the Gulph, and Lite could hammer weld with the best of them. Most important, Lite was willing to give his gun the time and attention that would make it a fine piece in every detail. There was no substitute for good workmanship. Lite knew that, and he stood ready to instill that quality in this gun—and in anything else he might ever decide to make. He always had.

Besides, for years men in both Europe and América had been looking for better and more accurate methods of making arms. It had been that way practically since the middle of the thirteenth century, when Friar Roger Bacon first recorded the formula for gunpowder. Lite was simply assuming his place in history. For, once the novelty of the "mysterious black powder" had worn off, it was quickly mated with a device that could put it to work—the gun—and together the two had reshaped civilization.

Days of chivalry and of gallant knights in

suits of mail came to a close, and victory in war became more and more dependent on the accuracy of a gun and the shooting skill of its owner. Where law and order did not exist, the gun provided authority. Particularly in colonial America, where the Indians showed European newcomers the advantages of hiding in a woodland and taking an adversary from a goodly distance, and where a settler often had to be able to hunt to provide meat for his table, guns had become important tools of survival. It seemed necessary to have the best gun that was available. Small wonder that, after giving the matter considerable thought, Lite Remington decided to go ahead—to try to make the best rifle ever made.

Eliphalet Remington, the Remington Arms Company founder

At the forge, he hammered the soft iron that he selected for the barrel, wrapping it around a rod to form the bore, and then welding it under the hammer with a flux of borax and sand to make the joint stick. Once he finished the rough work, he attacked the outside of the new barrel, first with a water-driven grindstone, then with a file, dressing it down and forming the flat faces of the much-admired octagonal form. Then he was stuck. He needed help. Any good blacksmith could forge a barrel and dress its exterior. The inside of the bore was another matter. That required special equipment, which only a professional gunsmith could afford.

So it was that young Remington set out for Utica, where he could obtain the help he needed. Tradition, often repeated as fact, says

15

Settler defending his children from Indian attack with flintlock

that he sought out a young gunsmith named Morgan James, who had a shop in that flourishing new metropolis. Since James was actually only three years old at the time, it seems that tradition must be wrong, and that Lite got his help from some other, less well known, gunsmith. This same tradition also says that Remington walked the whole distance, carrying the new barrel blank, as well as his father's rifle, for protection against panthers, lynxes, and other wild animals. But the Remingtons were a well-to-do-family with a successful farm, a blacksmith shop, and several other sources of income. It is much more likely that Lite took one of the farm horses and rode to town—and he probably didn't even need a gun to protect himself against wild animals. The chances of being attacked by a panther in broad daylight, while mounted on a horse, were mighty slim

A turkey shoot, old style, with live turkeys as targets

Long rifles, better known as the Kentucky rifles

even in those days. Still, it made a good story.

At the shop, the gunsmith examined Remington's barrel blank and agreed to ream and rifle it. The reaming came first, to smooth out the rough interior. Then each of the twisting rifle grooves was cut into the barrel with a hand-operated rifling machine. It was a long and tedious job. The reaming probably took less than two hours, but the rifling was a far more difficult task.

If, as he waited patiently for his own barrel to be rifled, Lite gave much thought to how or when the first rifled firearm was produced, he surely had no answers. The earliest guns, introduced in the fourteenth century, were smooth bores. Some scholars in Remington's century believed that rifles were in existence as early as 1476, but no evidence has ever been found to substantiate such a theory. Still, there

17

seems to be little doubt that the ancestors of this gun of Lite's date back at least to the mid-1500's. And it seems almost as likely that the first rifle to send its load spinning toward its mark was the result of considerable experimentation—rather than accident.

For years, arms makers had set feathers of arrows and crossbow bolts at an angle, so that they would spin in flight, and it was well known that spinning made them more stable as they passed through the air. So, even if the unknown inventor of the rifle was unaware of why a spinning ball or bullet flew straighter and struck harder—and no one did know until 1742, when Benjamin Robbins discovered and noted the scientific principles involved—early gunsmiths could recognize the superior performance rifling made possible.

Lite very probably did muse a bit about the famed Kentucky rifle. It was purely American. Some had called it the Pennsylvania rifle, because it was first produced by the German gunsmiths in Pennsylvania in the 1750's, and some called it the long rifle because of its graceful, elongated shape, totally unlike the short-barreled arms brought to the colonies from Europe. It was light and sturdy and supremely accurate and, in the colonies where powder was so precious, it offered smaller calibers that conserved both powder and shot. To make certain that their rifles wasted no powder, the

Rare, muzzle-loading Remington flintlock rifle, produced 1816 to 1846 in a variety of calibers. The flintlock shown on the gun is a replacement

frontiersmen often tested them over an expanse of fresh snow, decreasing the amount of powder used until no marks were left on the snow after the gun was discharged.

Exciting stories surrounded the Kentucky rifles. They had been carried by the Continentals in the American Revolution in the Battle of Kings Mountain. One British officer was even reported to have remarked that "provided an American rifleman were to get a perfect aim at 300 yards at me, standing still, he most undoubtedly would hit me, unless it was a very windy day. . . ."

The thought of making such a fine rifle had to be exciting to a young man with Lite's talent and imagination. It must have passed through his mind a score of times. But Lite was interested in mechanics of all kinds, and watching the gunsmith work diligently on his barrel must also have set Lite's brain working on ways to improve such wearisome methods. For while the machinery was effective, it was far from sophisticated.

A small cutting tooth on the end of a hickory rod cut each groove as it was pushed back and forth through the bore with a pre-set twisting motion controlled by an indexing guide. Every six or eight passes through the barrel, the cutting tooth was shifted so that it would cut the next groove. When all had been scratched lightly, a paper-thin shim was put under the

19

Ilion, New York, forge, where Remington Arms Company began

"Lite" Remington at the anvil at which he hammered his first gun

Portion of a gun-barrel coil, start of a barrel

tooth to make it protrude farther, and the process was begun again. It was continued for hours, until all the grooves had reached the desired depth. According to family tradition, the gunsmith charged Lite four double reales (about one dollar) for the job. Also, according to tradition, he was so impressed by Remington's work and his conversation that he gave him a lock to put on the gun.

Lite now had a lock for his gun, and the makings of a barrel, for the barrel still required some work. As it stood, it was just a simple rifled tube, open at both ends. Lite would have to forge a plug for it, cut threads so that it could be screwed into the breech end of the barrel, and close it. The breech plug also would hold the tang used to fasten the barrel to the stock, and, of course, Lite still needed a stock. Then there was the matter of sights. These, too, had to be made. The backsight was usually an open V forged from iron and keyed to the top of the barrel. The front sight was normally a blade made out of a soft, bright

20

Lockport, Erie Canal. Expansion westward, aided by the canal, produced a need for guns never before experienced in the U.S.

metal, such as pewter, brass, or occasionally silver. Often one could be filed out of a coin or token. Lite made all of these things. Then, when the barrel was all finished, he browned it, probably with a mixture of urine and iron oxide, to reduce glare when sighting and also to help prevent rust.

The stock was a relatively simple matter. The Remingtons undoubtedly had a number of straight-grained maple or walnut planks, well seasoned by months of storage in the rafters. If they had none, they could easily obtain one from a neighbor or the nearest sawmill. The stock of another gun could be traced for a pattern and sawed out; the barrel groove could then be scooped out with a gouge, the lock mortise cut with drill and chisel, and the final shape rendered with draw knife and rasp.

The hardware was another matter. Such

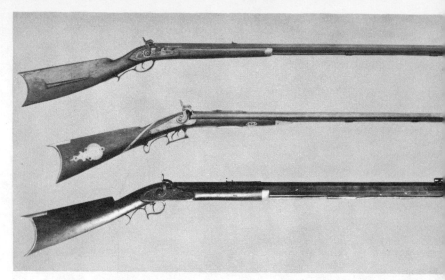

Above: half stock percussion lock rifle. Middle: percussion lock single-barrel shotgun. Bottom: percussion lock target rifle

things as butt plates, trigger guards, side plates and ramrod thimbles had to be cast. Many gunsmiths who were not equipped with foundry facilities bought such items from suppliers who specialized in them, and it is probable that this is just what Remington did. Perhaps he bought them in Utica.

Family tradition is silent on the source of young Remington's gun mountings, but it does relate that he finished assembling the new arm on a Saturday evening. There can be few urges as strong as the desire to try out a new gun, especially for a young man who has made the whole thing himself, and even more especially if it is the very first one he has ever made. Lite must have felt this urge intensely all day Sunday. But he was a devout Methodist, and not even an occasion like this could make him break the Sabbath by firing a gun. That had to wait for Monday.

When that day finally came, there was no **22** disappointment. The action worked smoothly;

Sporting gun with a double barrel—with one barrel rifled for .45 caliber, the other in .32 gauge. The weight was about eleven pounds

the gun shot true. Lite had been right—he could indeed make a gun, and had proved it by making a very fine one.

Just how fine a gun it was, he demonstrated that autumn. After harvest was in, there was a slack time for country folk. With the crops in, they turned to general repair and maintenance jobs about the farm, but they also had time to play. This was the season for social gatherings and for contests of skill, and one of the most popular of all such contests was a rifle match. There were many kinds of these matches. Usually there was an entry fee, and often the marksmen might fire for a share of the pot. Sometimes the sponsor of the match bought and butchered a steer, and the contestants vied for choice cuts from it. There were also turkey shoots, with a live bird staked down behind a log as the shooters tried to get it to expose its head for a target. Such turkey shoots reached their real popularity a bit later, however. In Lite's time, the usual target was a shingle or **23**

Maynard tape lock shown open at bottom, and closed

board with a cross or circle marked on it, and the winner was the man who could fire off-hand and place the most shots closest to dead center.

In just such a fall contest, after he had finished his new rifle, Remington managed to win second prize, beating all but one of the best shots in the county. Family reminiscences relate that, when it was over, the winner asked Lite if he could try his new rifle and was so delighted with it he then and there asked Remington if he could make one for him also. Lite reckoned he would. Other shooters crowded around and asked for rifles or rifle barrels also and, before he knew it, Remington was in the gun business. The year was 1816.

These early Remington arms were all custom made. Whatever a customer asked for he got, be it rifle or shotgun, full-stock or half-stock. The barrels might be soft iron, steel, or "stub twist"—that is, made up of strips of iron and steel twisted together, wrapped spirally around a rod and welded. Stub twist barrels were also called "Damascus" barrels, and they were both strong and popular. In a few years there were pistols also, the first sale of a handgun being recorded in 1835, though some may well have been made earlier. A few of these early Remington guns have survived to show what they were like and to indicate the high quality of materials and workmanship that characterized the product.

The earliest of these Remingtons were probably flintlocks, since this was the most popu-

24

Hammer, nipple mechanism of old-time percussion lock

Pull of the trigger released hammer to the percussion cap

lar ignition system of the day. The flintlock itself was a simple device. It was merely a mechanical version of the operation the average householder performed every day when he lighted a fire by striking flint and steel together. In the gun lock, the piece of flint was held in a clamp on the end of a pivoted arm called a cock. This would correspond to the hammer on a more recent gun. Opposite it was a piece of steel fastened to the lid of a little pan that the shooter carefully filled with fine gunpowder before each shot.

When he pulled the trigger, the cock, impelled by a strong spring, swung forward and struck the steel a sharp, raking blow. This not only produced a shower of sparks but also knocked the steel back and so opened the lid of the little pan and exposed the priming powder in it. The sparks ignited the priming powder, and the resulting flash passed through a hole in the side of the barrel to set off the main charge inside. The description is long, but in actual practice the whole procedure took only a second or so from the pull of the trigger to the ignition of the charge.

It was a vast improvement over the locks

25

The matchlock, invented at the end of the fifteenth century, had a wick which had to be lighted in order to fire the weapon

that had preceded it. The matchlock, one of the first great advancements in gunmaking, came in the latter part of the fifteenth century and was used for some two centuries afterward. But it had several drawbacks, and these became particularly obvious when the lock was carried to the New World in 1539 by Hernando de Soto and his small army of explorers and treasure seekers. True, the matchlock required far less motion for the shooter to fire his weapon than had earlier ignition systems, and it freed him to steady his hold and perfect his aim. It was also relatively inexpensive to produce, and simple enough in principle for a layman to repair. It had worked fine in Europe, where fighting was generally a formal affair, carried on in fair weather on an open field.

But in America, conditions were different. Colonials found the wheel lock a far more suitable device. It was rugged and dependable, eliminated the problem of the telltale match, and would even work in wind or light rain. Best of all, it could be kept ready to fire at all times, and concealed without fear of accidental discharge. However, the wheel lock, too, had its disadvantages.

Explorer de Soto preferred his sword to a matchlock

Its principle of producing sparks by rubbing stone against steel was simple enough, but its method of creating the reaction was extremely complex. As many as thirty-five to fifty parts went into a fully developed wheel lock, and this, plus the workmanship involved, made it extremely expensive to produce. In addition, if it developed trouble, it required an expert to repair it—a very unfortunate set of circumstances in the midst of a battle or if its owner were being charged by a "b'ar."

The flintlock used in Lite's rifle was much more dependable, and it operated faster than it can be described, yet it too had its serious drawbacks. There was a delay, noticeable to any shooter, between the trigger pull and the explosion, and its system was susceptible to dampness. It just wouldn't work in a heavy rain. A new ignition system, based on an explosive compound that detonated when it was struck, had been invented in 1807 by a Scottish clergyman named Alexander John Forsyth, but it took many years to develop a method of using it that was practical for such a backwoods community as the Gulph.

Not long after Remington started his business, such a method, the percussion cap, had come into use, and it is a good guess that many

27

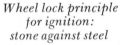

*Wheel lock principle
for ignition:
stone against steel*

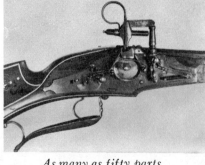

*As many as fifty parts
were needed for the
wheel lock mechanism*

of Remington's guns were being made for the
new cap very early in his career. The percussion lock was simpler than the flintlock. The
cock was replaced by a hammer, and the old
steel and pan gave way to a simple tube, called
a nipple, leading to the inside of the bore. The
shooter simply cocked the hammer, placed a
percussion cap on the nipple, and pulled the
trigger. The reaction was almost instantane-
ous. The old lag was gone, and the new cap
was almost impervious to moisture. It was a
good system, and Remington stuck with it for
many years.

A successful gun-making business is more
than a one-man operation. Even before the end
of 1816, Eliphalet Remington II had help. His
father supported the new business and took
an active part in its management, and a skilled
gunsmith named Riley Rogers soon started to
work on forging, grinding, reaming, and rifling. New facilities were added at the Gulph
and, almost as soon, they were outgrown. In
1828 the Remingtons decided to move down to
the bank of the new Erie Canal. There they
would have easy access to water transportation

Stop-action photograph of the wheel lock in action. An enormous improvement over the matchlock, it produced its own spark

for their products, which were finding an ever-widening market. That year they built a new and modern factory — and suffered a tragedy, when the elder Remington was killed in a wagon accident.

But the start had been made. The new factory increased in size and the number of workmen grew yearly. Soon there was a flourishing community around the plant, which many of the residents wanted to call Remington's Corners. Lite would have none of this, however. It smacked too much of personal vanity for his God-fearing soul, and he forced through the name of Ilion, in keeping with the other classical designations given such up-and-coming nearby communities as Troy, Utica, Syracuse.

29

CHAPTER TWO

MAGIC WORDS ON THE BARREL

Once it took raw courage to be
an artillerist, but two short
words made all the difference

MAGIC WORDS ON THE BARREL

A custom gun shop, even a very good one, is a limited operation. A man who had contemplated becoming a poet in his youth naturally thinks of bigger things and wider opportunities. Eliphalet Remington had laid aside his poetic aspirations when he had entered the gun business, but he still had dreams. He wanted to offer fine firearms to the sportsmen, farmers and householders of America at a price that any of them could afford. He could not do this within the framework of his present business. He could go ahead and make popular types of guns on speculation, when his men were not fully employed in working to specific orders from dealers or private customers, but even this would not do the trick. Output would still remain small and costs would have to stay relatively high. What he needed was a really big order that would allow him to build and install the machines necessary to put quality workmanship on a production-line basis. Once he had done that, he could offer the very best of guns at a reasonable price. A poetic aspiration could be achieved. The problem was to find the order.

The opportunity Remington sought was slow in coming, but when it did, he was quick to recognize it and to take advantage of it. Unlikely as it might have seemed, his chance sprang from a government contract offered to

Preceding page, left to right: Merrill carbine, Jenks carbine, Remington "Zouave" rifle, converted Harpers Ferry musket, Maynard tape lock

someone else. On December 5, 1842, the Ordnance Department had awarded a contract for 5,000 model 1841 percussion rifles to John Griffiths of Cincinnati, Ohio. The government was paying 13 dollars apiece for these rifles, and when Griffiths failed to make deliveries as called for, Remington jumped at the chance to take over the job. The longed-for machinery was installed. Workers were hired, and soon Remington was producing the military rifles at a rate of 1,000 a month. They were good rifles, too, and Ordnance was sufficiently pleased to order an additional 7,500.

William Jenks, the designer of the Jenks carbine

There is an old saying that it never rains but it pours. So it seemed to Remington. After waiting years for the opportunity to expand through one military contract, he suddenly found himself in the midst of another. In his search for machines, men and materials to complete the Griffiths contract, Lite visited the foundry and factories of N. P. Ames, near Springfield, Massachusetts. There he found the workmen busily manufacturing a new and ingenious firearm. It was a breechloader invented by William Jenks of Columbia, South Carolina, that had been ordered in small quantities for the Navy and for the Army.

Remington was intrigued with the gun. Its design appealed to his mechanical interests. There was a lever lying along the wrist of the stock and terminating on top of the breech. When this lever was raised and pulled back, it exposed a hole in the breech. At the same time, it slid a breech bolt back from its posi-

33

*A Remington-Jenks
rifled carbine with
Maynard tape lock*

tion just below the hole, so that the aperture now led directly into the bore of the gun. A bullet could be dropped in the hole, followed by a charge of powder, and as the lever was pushed back down it shoved the breech bolt forward, pushing the load into the chamber and sealing the breech. It was a good strong action. No Jenks breech failed in any of the severe tests given it by the Army and Navy ordnance boards. The Jenks also had another interesting feature. It was a mule ear—that is, the nipple for the percussion cap stuck out of the side of the barrel instead of pointing upwards, and the hammer moved sideways instead of up and down as most other gun hammers did.

All in all, it was a fascinating firearm. The Ames Company was having some second thoughts about its entry into firearms making, and so Remington decided to do business on the spot. When he left, he owned the rights to the Jenks system, the machinery for making it, the balance of the government contract, and the services of William Jenks himself. It was a considerable deal, and both parties were delighted with it.

Remington now was the sole supplier of the only mule ear and the only sliding breech bolt firearm ever issued to American troops, and he proceeded with attempts to improve it. For one thing, he added a Maynard tape primer so that the shooter would not have to place a percussion cap on the nipple each time he fired. The Maynard primer worked like the roll of caps in a modern toy pistol, with little

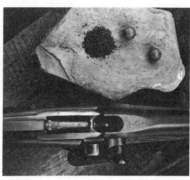

The mule ear, in which hammer moved sideways when released

Jenks carbine, barrel of cast steel, shown with its powder and ball

charges of detonating compound in a long strip of tape. Each time the hammer was cocked the tape advanced and another primer moved over the nipple, making the priming process automatic.

More important was another improvement that did not even show, except for the two words CAST STEEL stamped on the top of the barrel. Previously, all small arms barrels had been forged around a rod called a mandrel, either in a spiral for the Damascus or stub twist barrel or as a flat sheet, which was trough welded in a single seam, for the commoner barrels. The cast steel barrels provided shooters with safer and more reliable guns.

With the Jenks carbine, Remington pioneered a new method of making gun barrels: a solid steel rod was placed in a machine and bored from end to end. Cannon tubes had been drilled for years, but they had proportionally shorter bores, thicker barrel walls. It was a difficult task to bore a hole through a slender rod some forty inches long and keep the hole from coming out one side. It was even

35

Forge in Ilion quickly expanded into an armory

Philo Remington, one of three sons born to Eliphalet

more difficult to make that hole absolutely straight, as it had to be for a successful gun barrel. But the Remington factory had succeeded early in the 1840's, and their boring machines were ready for the large scale production when the Jenks contract arrived.

Despite its apparent advantages, the Jenks breechloader never became popular. Ordnance officials seemed to be either steadfast adherents of John Hall's earlier breechloading system or else dead set against any arm that loaded from the rear. The Jenks performed well in tests. One board of testing officers went so far as almost to recommend it for those fighting men who would find it difficult to use a ramrod and load through the muzzle, and they specifically mentioned sailors in the fighting tops of war ships and dragoons on horseback. The Terry and Westley Richards carbines, which used a sliding breech bolt similar to the Jenks, became very popular in England, but Remington sold a relatively small number of his breechloaders to the government and not many more to sportsmen. Still, he did have the machinery, which could

36

be adapted for making other sorts of guns, and this was a factor which gladdened his heart.

Eliphalet Remington had something else to be happy about. First one son and then all three joined him in the business, and they were showing natural aptitudes for the work, particularly Philo, who was a mechanic at heart and took naturally to gunsmithing. He entered the business in 1844. Eliphalet III, too, was a good if not distinguished workman and an excellent accountant. And then there was Sam. A *bon vivant* who shunned the strict temperance creed of his ancestors, Sam was a natural salesman. He spent much of his time supervising the distribution of Remington guns throughout the country and the world, obtaining contracts and generally overseeing the outside affairs of the firm, which was now known proudly as E. Remington & Sons.

Despite his contract work on the model 1841

Remington Armory, Ilion, New York, in mid 1800's

37

Civil War soldiers, standing with rifles of the day: the rifles are equipped with saber bayonets

Popular war rifle —the Remington "Zouave" of 1862

rifle and the Jenks carbine, Remington had not neglected the civilian sportsman, the man whom Lite always considered his most important customer and for whom he had sought the extra machinery. Throughout the relatively quiet decade of the fifties, he expanded his line of guns and developed new sales outlets, including the well known firm of Schuyler, Hartley & Graham.

In 1861 the days of peace were over. The sportsman and his interests could no longer command top priority. The tools of war were needed as never before in the history of the nation, and the firm of E. Remington & Sons, as well as all the other gun manufacturers, had to devote full time to producing military arms. Government contracts poured in—for the new revolvers, for bayonets, for gun locks, and for gun accessories of all sorts. There was a special demand for the standard rifles and rifle muskets. These were the basic small arms of the war, and Remington promptly tooled up to produce them as needed. They were the

By taking New Bern and Roanoke Island (above), the North was able to open the way for a sea-borne invasion against the South

last muzzle-loading rifles that Remington was to produce.

The order for the rifles came first—12,500 in all—and it is possible to trace the efforts of the factory to get into production by studying the changes in the guns as they were finished. The contract was signed July 30, 1861, just nine days after the disastrous Union defeat at First Bull Run, and it called for 10,000 rifles. After years of making peaceful sporting arms, however, Remington was not ready for the sudden demand. Lite made every effort—and died just a month later in the midst of his exertions. His

A sketch by Davenport from "Harper's Weekly" of General Sigel's Corps at the second battle of Bull Run, fought in August 1862

sons immediately kept up the pressure to get the new rifles into production. To start, they used some of the machinery originally acquired for the model 1841 rifles to cut seven deep rifling grooves into the bore. Later they were able to set up other rifling machines and cut the new type of rifling, with only three shallow grooves, that was the current vogue in military rifles. Instead of iron hardware, the Remingtons used brass. It was a little more expensive, but it could be cast more quickly and easily than the usual iron buttplates and barrel bands could be fabricated. Just incidentally, it also made the rifles handsomer to look at. It was a fine gun for the 17 dollar price Ordnance agreed to pay. A new contract

40

The Merrill carbine was made to use a rim-fire cartridge rather than loose powder and a ball

of August 11, 1862, covered these changes, and because of it many collectors call this Remington rifle the model 1862. Others called it the Remington Zouave rifle, and reproductions of it are being made and sold today under both names. Neither name was ever official. The 1862 contract and the one for an additional 2,500, which followed on December 13, 1863, refer only to "rifles with sword bayonets."

The Remington rifle, with its brass furniture and handsome appearance, is known to collectors far and wide. Fewer collectors are familiar with the Remington rifle musket, yet the firm made 40,000 of them during the war. This model was similar to the rifle of the period, only it was longer—the standard musket length of 56 inches, rather than the 49 inches of the traditionally shorter rifle. Also, it took an angular socket bayonet instead of the unwieldy saber bayonet. More model 1861 rifle muskets saw action than any other single model. Many were made at the Springfield Armory. Remington's 40,000 made a substantial contribution to the war effort, even without the other necessary weapons, which the plant at Ilion was turning out on an almost round-the-clock schedule.

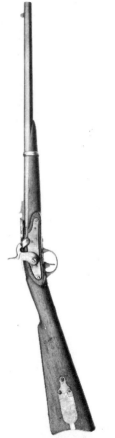

Merrill carbine of 1856-1861; weight: 6 pounds

CHAPTER THREE

THE REVOLVERS THAT WENT WEST

George Armstrong Custer's hand gun was specially made, with his portrait on the ivory grip

THE REVOLVERS THAT WENT WEST

Single-shot rifles, shotguns and rifle muskets were fine for infantrymen, hunters and marksmen who did their shooting on foot. Remington had specialized in meeting the desires of all three. But Lite had not ignored other needs. He was interested in providing a personal defense weapon for the average householder or storekeeper, for the traveler who wanted a convenient gun to stash under the seat of his wagon, and for the horseman who needed a firearm he could carry with him in a holster or in his saddle bags. Central New York state was a calm and peaceful area, but crime was not unknown. There was some need for such personal arms even there. Besides, Remington guns were already traveling far and wide into much more lawless and unsettled regions, and the demand for an easily carried firearm was tremendous.

These people needed pistols, not long guns, and Remington was sensitive to their desires. Pistol barrels and complete pistols had appeared in his sales records from an early date, made to order whenever a customer asked for one. These were single-shot weapons, sufficient for many emergencies. But Lite knew there was something better.

This better pistol was a revolver. Back in 1836, Sam Colt had demonstrated that a successful percussion revolver could be manufac-

Preceding page, left to right: the Beals Army revolver, single action, .44 caliber; model 1861 .36 caliber Navy; New Model .44 caliber Army

tured in quantity. True, Colt had gone bankrupt in a few years, but this had been due to the substantial costs of establishing a new business and trying to obtain sufficiently big contracts to keep it going. Remington was already a large, established firm with a substantial backlog of capital to carry it through the difficult period of waiting for a new kind of arm to catch on. That waiting period would not be so long, for the early Colt revolvers had continued to win friends even after the manufacturing company had folded. Now Colt was back in business with every indication that he would last this time. Lite made up his mind he wanted to make a revolver, too, but first he had to wait until Colt's basic patent had expired, and then he had to find a revolver of a new design that would be worth manufacturing. Time alone took care of one of these problems. To solve the other, he had to find a gun designer with a gun he would sell.

Taking pistol practice the day before a duel

It seemed like the answer to a prayer when Fordyce Beals arrived on the scene and agreed to let Remington manufacture a revolver he had just designed. Beals was not a newcomer to the revolver field. He already had had one such gun of his design manufactured by the Eli Whitney armory in 1854 and 1855. It had not been a success, but Beals thought he knew why, and he had redesigned the arm to overcome the difficulties as he saw them. Remington believed he had solved the problems too. They signed an agreement, and in 1857 Remington began to produce its first revolver.

45

Presentation revolvers. Top to bottom: M/1875 Army; New Model pocket conversion; Navy cartridge model; New Line; M/1890 Army

This first Remington-Beals was a pocket weapon, designed entirely for civilian use. Early advertising circulars declared that "The Compactness, Lightness and Simplicity of this Arm, together with the Size of the Ball, Range and Penetration, make it one of the most Convenient and Reliable Weapons of Defence that can be found." It was indeed a light, easily carried gun, weighing only 11 ounces, and firing a .31 caliber ball. It offered five shots ready for instant use, and Remington advised customers to buy an extra cylinder that could be carried along loaded and ready to be inserted quickly if more shots were needed in a hurry. Finished pistols were offered in cardboard boxes complete with a brass bullet mold, a copper powder flask, and a brass bullet seater. Spe-

46

"Drunken Cow-Boy on the 'War-Path' "—in the Wild West, such scenes were common occurrences

cial wooden cases were also supplied on order.

Success was no more prompt in recognizing this revolver of Beals' than it had his first attempt. Collectors estimate that 2,500 to 3,000 were made. Then Beals redesigned his gun. A sheath trigger replaced the usual trigger and guard, and made the piece more streamlined, while the top of the frame over the cylinder was straightened and the grips were changed to a more conventional shape.

Probably 1,000 of these "second model" Beals were made and then, in 1859, Beals redesigned once again. This time he increased the size of the revolver considerably, lengthening the barrel from three inches to four and adding a loading lever so that the separate and easily lost bullet seater of the first two models was no longer needed. The extra length and the lever jumped the weight of this "third model" Beals to 14 ounces, but it remained a light gun, and it was much more convenient

Beals revolving rifle, 6 shot cap and ball, 1858

Top to bottom: Old Model Army; early experimental revolver; 1890 Army presentation; Iroquois presentation; New Line No. 3

than the earlier models. Still, only about 1,500 were made before production ceased in 1860.

Of all three models made since 1857, Remington had been able to produce and sell only about 5,000 or 6,000 revolvers. Had it been a new company, relying solely on this market for existence, it surely would have failed just as Colt had. Here Remington had the advantage. Other phases of the business could carry the revolvers while Lite sought the superior model he knew he could make, through a few more years, while customer demand for that model developed.

Remington decided to try something bigger, to leave the pocket category and develop

New Line revolver, cased, was made from 1877 to 1885

The Remington New Model Navy percussion revolver; hand-carved grips, cased accessories

Sam Colt, pioneer of the revolving-cylinder handgun

a large revolver for a horseman to carry in a holster or thrust through his belt. Beals had just developed and patented a new type of loading lever and cylinder pin, and at Lite's suggestion he incorporated them into a brand new revolver model. Not only would it be longer and heavier than the pocket models, but it would have a bigger caliber as well.

There were two standard calibers for holster pistols at that time, the .44 and the .36. The Army had long favored the .44 size, and it had come to be known as the Army caliber, while the Navy had adopted the .36. Actually both services used pistols of both calibers, and there were numerous .44 and .36 revolvers that were never used by either service, but which soon came to be called "Army" or "Navy" pistols solely because of their caliber. This happened to the big Beals revolvers. None were bought by the government, but collectors today refer

49

Clockwise from the bottom: Frank and Jesse James, Cole Younger and Bob Younger

to the Beals Army and the Beals Navy pistols.

The big Beals revolvers were just the beginning. In 1861, slightly improved versions of both were designed and manufactured, and these actually were purchased by the United States for use during the Civil War. Then, in 1863, further improvements produced the "New Model" Army and Navy revolvers, which found extremely wide popularity. One hundred and seventy-two thousand of the two models were made and sold between the date of their introduction and 1875, when they gave way to cartridge models.

George Armstrong Custer owned a specially engraved example, with his portrait carved in relief on its ivory grips. Many other officers and countless enlisted men also carried the Remington New Model and prized it for its sturdiness, safety and fine shooting qualities. Cole Younger carried one when he rode with Quantrill's guerrillas, and he kept it during his outlaw days after the war. It was a fine gun. The solid frame over the cylinder gave it a solidity that many of its competitors lacked, and the sighting groove milled out of this top strap provided a far surer aim than the notch filed in a moving part, such as the hammer, which was what many other revolvers were reduced to offering. Colt, which had the early start in the field and which also produced

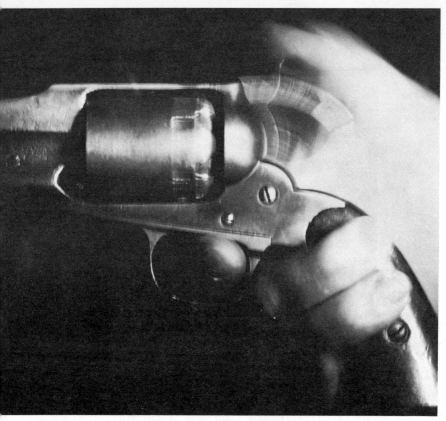

The revolver proved to be one of the most successful innovations in gun making. Light in weight, it offered six rapid shots

excellent guns, supplied more revolvers for the Civil War than any other company. Remington, with only a few years' experience, was second. Today, many of the country's most experienced shooters of muzzle-loading revolvers consider the Remington New Model the finest percussion revolver ever made.

After the Civil War, the big Remington revolvers went West. Cowboy, lawman, outlaw and just plain citizen in that wild country liked the sturdy revolvers with their sure aim. As metal-cased cartridges came into general use, Remington was quick to adapt to them,

51

Beals pocket revolver, Second Model, offering 5 shots, .31 caliber, with a German silver cone sight

and with few changes the New Model Armys and Navys became cartridge guns in 1875.

Back in 1859, Lite had heard of an unusual double-action revolver patented by Joseph Rider out in Newark, Ohio. Right away he was intrigued. Most revolvers then being made, including the Beals, were single-action —that is, the hammer had to be pulled back with the thumb before the trigger could be pulled. In Rider's new revolver, a single pull of the trigger rotated the cylinder, cocked the hammer and then released it to fire the gun. It was simpler and much faster. This sort of improvement was just the thing that Remington wanted to be able to offer, and he lost no time in obtaining the rights to the new pistol and in getting the services of Rider himself, since he suspected that young man might well make some more contributions to gun design and wanted Remington to be in a position to manufacture them. The Rider revolver was a

52

The Rider Pocket Revolver. Caliber: .31. Barrel: 3" octagon. With large oval, brass trigger guard

good purchase. It sold well, both in its original form as a percussion cap weapon, and later as a cartridge arm. It kept a production line busy until 1888 as 100,000 were manufactured.

Other revolvers followed. In 1873, Remington brought out its New Line cartridge revolvers with their famous one-piece barrel and frame, which not only gave them great strength, but also made them less expensive to make. There were four models, ranging from a small .30 caliber through .32 to a hefty .38, large for a pocket model.

The last Remington revolver was a single-action Army model, which very much resembled the Colt. The company brought it out in 1891, and manufactured some 2,000. Unlike most Remington arms, however, it had little new and superior to offer. It was good, but no better than the Colt. It disappeared in 1894, and with it Remington abandoned the revolver field after 37 years of success.

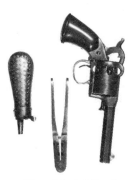

First Model Beals pocket revolver was a .31 caliber

53

CHAPTER FOUR

FABULOUS LITTLE HAND GUNS

For a time, no self-respecting dandy would be without one of these fashionable weapons of defense

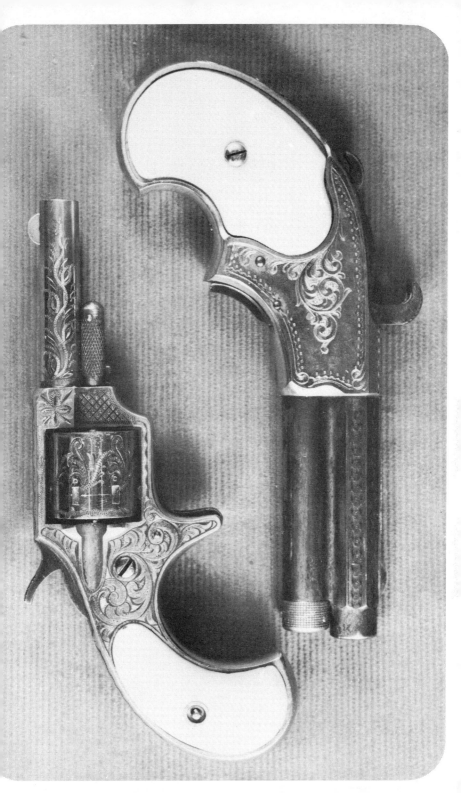

FABULOUS LITTLE HAND GUNS

A revolver is a sizeable weapon. Even a little pocket model with a 3-inch barrel, like the Beals, makes a noticeable bulge. In a day when law-abiding citizens would not venture on the streets of many cities at night without a firearm, when professional gamblers would just as soon have been caught without their cards as without some form of defense, and when congressmen sometimes carried pistols into the United States Capitol, these were major considerations. Henry Deringer, Jr., had proved just how popular a little pistol could be. He had become famous from producing one, and had given his name to a class of weapons.

Here was a need and a market that Remington could not overlook. Lite tried it first with a little .17 caliber percussion cap pistol designed by Joseph Rider, whom Remington had originally brought to Ilion because of his double-action revolver. Rider's pistol was small and inconspicuous, all right. The trouble was, it was too small to be any good.

It was the younger Remingtons who really developed the pocket pistol market. After Lite's death in the summer of 1861, Philo, Sam and the third Eliphalet brought out little pistols in a profusion of models.

Key man in the development of many of the Remington pocket pistols was William H. Elliot, of Plattsburg, New York.

Preceding page, right: Rider magazine pistol, .32 caliber, rim fire extra short; left: the Iroquois revolver, .22 caliber, with a seven shot capacity

What Elliot succeeded in doing was to design a cartridge repeating pistol in tiny pocket size. In so doing, he harked back to the old pepperbox arms, with their cluster of barrels, that had preceded the cylinder revolvers. Because there was no gap between cylinder and barrel on such guns, there was none of the distressing loss of power that always plagued true revolvers. For this reason, smaller cartridges could be used, and they would still hit hard. Elliot enclosed the hammers on his pistols so that there would be no projection to take up room or to get caught in the folds of a pocket just when the owner wanted to pull his pistol out in a hurry. Elliot also made his pistols with ring triggers and a form of double action for both speed and safety. The first of these pocket repeaters had zig-zag lines cut into the sides of its barrel block. For this reason, collectors today call it the zig-zag derringer. Remington called it a pocket repeater or a revolver—the latter because the barrel block revolved. When the shooter pushed the ring trigger forward, it cocked the hammer and rotated the barrels to bring a fresh charge into firing position. When he pulled the trigger back, it fired the gun.

Only a few of these little 6-shot pistols were made in 1861 and 1862, all .22 caliber. Then Elliot's improved version came out. The new pistol offered fewer shots—five in the .22 caliber size and only four in the .32—but it was a sturdier arm. In this version, the barrels remained stationary and the firing pin rotated. Here was a fine, hard-shooting weapon that

Vest pocket pistol, .22 caliber, rimfire, single shot

57

Experimental vest pocket pistol—stock was detachable

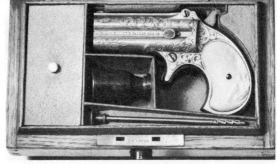

Remington double derringer, depending on type of model, offered .32 or .22 rim fire and 4 or 5 shots

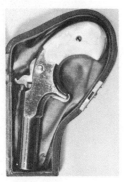

The Elliot single-shot derringer, .41 caliber rim fire

offered enough shots to take care of most emergencies and still weighed only ounces.

The Elliot pocket repeaters offered power and multiple shots in just about the smallest imaginable size. But the Remingtons still had in mind the customer who wanted even less of a bulge in his pocket, and would therefore settle for fewer shots. In 1865, they brought out another tiny single shot pistol, somewhat reminiscent of the old Rider in shape but this time a cartridge model firing a .22 rim fire shell. Remington called it a vest pocket pistol, and indeed it would fit into any of the pockets in a gentleman's waistcoat with never a wrinkle. It was almost completely flat. It would also fit into a lady's muff—or perhaps the top of a stocking. In any event, there were enough possible receptacles for it to account for sales of another 50,000 of the little pistols.

"How an investigation instituted by a passenger on a New York street car brought a young woman to the front like a little man."

Despite the success of the pocket repeaters and the vest pocket models, however, their combined sales totals could not touch the most famous of all Remington concealable weapons. This was Elliot's fabulous double derringer, patented on December 12, 1865, and marketed first in 1866. Here was a gun that built legends across the length and breadth of America. Lawmen and outlaws of the West found it the perfect hideout gun, to be used as a spare if their obvious six-shooter should be taken from them. It could be tucked in the sweatband of a hat, fastened around the neck, carried under the arm, thrust in a boot, or carried in a pocket. A man had to be checked very thoroughly if the searcher wanted to be sure not to overlook so small a weapon.

It was not only the diminutive size of the double derringer that made it popular. After

59

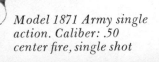

Model 1871 Army single action. Caliber: .50 center fire, single shot

Left to right: two Elliot 5-barreled, .22 caliber derringers, Elliot 4-barreled ring trigger derringer

Rider magazine pistol and the Rider cane gun

all, it was no smaller than the vest pocket pistols. Its really endearing qualities lay in the fact that it offered two powerful .41 caliber shots instead of the single round that the vest pocket model could produce. One extra shot may not seem like a great deal, but it often means the difference between success and failure, between life and death. The double derringer gave these two shots with the aid of two barrels, arranged one above the other to retain a flat silhouette. A firing pin, which moved when the hammer was cocked, fired first one barrel and then the other. To load, the shooter simply released a latch on the right hand side of the piece and tipped up the barrels, which were hinged on their upper edge. Although this was probably not the designer's original intention, the double derringer could also be used as a pair of "knucks" by grasping the barrels with the grips sticking out below the

60

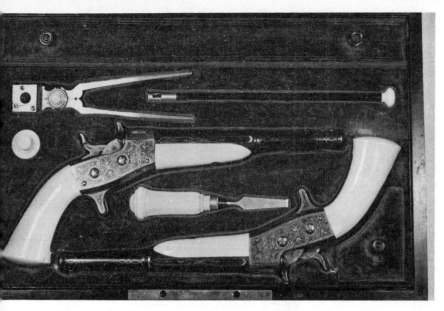

Cased model 1866 Navy pistols, single action. The caliber: .50 rim fire, single shot. Rifling: 3 grooves. Weight 2 pounds, 4 ounces

hand and the trigger between the second and third fingers.

Production of Elliot's double derringer began in 1866 and continued without interruption right up until 1935 — a remarkable 69 years. No other handgun in American history has been in production for so long a time.

Even after this success, Elliot kept steadily at work designing little pistols. In 1867, Remington brought out his tiny .41 caliber single-shot pistol, which was the ultimate in simplicity of design. Then, in 1871, they offered his magazine repeating pistols, with five .32 cartridges fed from a tubular magazine under the barrel. Both did reasonably well, selling some 10,000-15,000 each before production ceased, along with most other Remington pistols, in 1888. The double derringer kept on, however, to build an unchallenged record in the annals of American firearms manufacture. **61**

CHAPTER FIVE

THE SIOUX AND THE ROLLING BLOCK

Red Cloud and Crazy Horse couldn't understand it—these "white eyes" weren't taking time to reload

THE SIOUX AND THE ROLLING BLOCK

Fordyce Beals, Joseph Rider and William Elliot all gathered at the Remington plant in the 1850's and '60's. This was truly a talented assemblage of gun designers—one of the most gifted ever gathered in the United States—and they produced some fine firearms to bear the Remington name. But they were not the only ones, for to the list must be added the name of Leonard M. Geiger.

Philo Remington had found Geiger in the nearby city of Hudson, New York, where he had just developed an interesting breechloader, patenting it in 1863. Unlike any other breechloader of the time, this one had a pivoted breechblock that could be rolled backwards after the hammer had been cocked, thus exposing the chamber. Philo liked the idea so well that he persuaded Geiger to come to Ilion and work with the group of young gun designers already gathered there. It was a great stroke of luck that Philo sought Geiger and that Geiger agreed to come. From his association with Joseph Rider stemmed the great Remington rolling block action, perhaps the finest single-shot action of its time.

Like Philo, Rider also was intrigued with Geiger's breechloader from the moment he saw it. Soon he had ideas for changing and improving it with little refinements. Before the year was out, he had patented a system for in-

---

Preceding page: Remington rolling block rifle. Invented by Geiger, Rider and Remington, this was a fast, simple and very strong action

THE SIOUX AND THE ROLLING BLOCK

terlocking the hammer and breechblock so that the two worked against each other to form an especially strong breech when pressure was exerted against them from inside the barrel. A year later, in November 1864, Rider took out a patent on a different form of the rolling breechblock. This time it was a split block, with a hammer nose passing through it to detonate the cartridge. The group now thought they had a completely developed firearm, and the Remington brothers offered it to the government as a possible rifle for the Civil War. Ordnance also liked the system and contracted for some 20,000 of the rifles, some in .46 caliber, some in .50. Deliveries could not be made until March 1865, however, and the war ended in April, before any could be tested in action.

Meanwhile, Geiger and Rider were still busily improving their gun. By January, they had another model ready. It proved to have flaws, so they promptly returned to their drawing boards and soon had another version. By the winter of 1865-1866, the system was finally perfected, though further improvements were patented in April 1866, August 1867 and November 1871. It was a characteristic of the Remington design team that they were never satisfied; always they looked for some way to smooth an action, to strengthen a breech.

When they were finally happy with it, the rolling block breech was as simple, as strong and as nearly foolproof as an action could be. The shooter's motions remained the same as they had with Geiger's very first version, of

An early buffalo hunter in authentic dress

A side view of rolling block action, less stock

1863. First he cocked the hammer. Then, with his thumb, he rolled back the breechblock and exposed the opening into the bore. If he had already fired a shot, this action also extracted the spent cartridge case. In this position the new load was inserted, while one of the mechanical refinements worked out by Geiger and Rider locked the hammer in the cocked position and prevented a pinched finger or accidental discharge. Once the new cartridge was inserted, the shooter rolled the breechblock back into place, and the gun was ready to fire.

The old interlocking system of hammer and breechblock invented by Geiger still operated —and it had been strengthened even further. It was literally impossible to blow out a Remington rolling block breech with any ammunition available at the time. And there were people who tried! At the famous Belgian proof house in Liège, for instance, they loaded a .50 caliber rolling block solidly from breech to muzzle. They put in 750 grains of black powder and 40 bullets plus two wads. Then they fired it, and the director of the test noted calmly that "nothing extraordinary occurred." Other testers tried more imaginative ways to blow out a breech. They used tight-fitting balls, varied the proportion of powder to shot —and sometimes they even left a ramrod in the

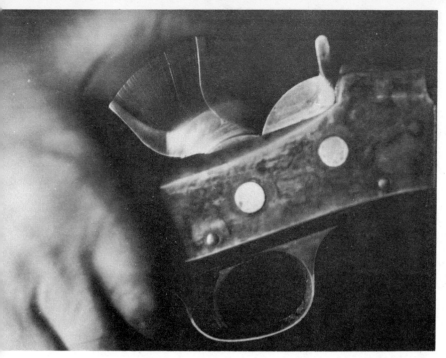

*The rolling block in action. When the breechblock was rolled
back, it extracted a spent cartridge case and exposed the chamber*

barrel. They also filed the cartridges so they
would burst in the chamber, but no one ever
succeeded in blowing the breech back or even
cracking the block.

Outside the proof houses of the United
States and Europe, the rolling block performed just as well as it had under test conditions. The saga of Nelson Story, for instance,
is well known to all students of American western lore. Story was a cowboy, a man of great
courage and even greater determination. Story
had struck it rich at Virginia City and had
invested a sizeable portion of his fortune in a
herd of 3,000 Texas cattle that he proposed to
drive all the way from the Lone Star State to
Montana. There he hoped to found a cattle
industry and increase his wealth. With the

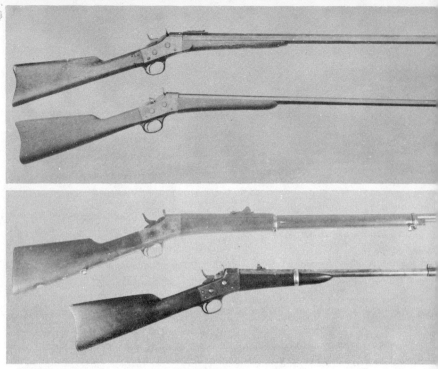

Top to bottom: sporting rifle No. 1, Remington-Rider shotgun No. 1, Model 1872 rolling block, Remington-Geiger rolling block

help of thirty Texas cowhands, he set out. Every man carried one or two revolvers, some of them Colts, some Remingtons. Story himself is said to have had two of the big Remington-Beals.

By the summer of 1866, they had reached Fort Leavenworth in Kansas. There they heard bad news. It seemed that Red Cloud and his Sioux were on the warpath. If Story was going to get his cattle to Montana he had to go right through their territory. He pressed on, but before he did he bought his men thirty new Remington rolling blocks that had just arrived in a shipment from the East.

The next part of the trip was uneventful. Story reached Fort Laramie in present-day

THE SIOUX AND THE ROLLING BLOCK

Wyoming without misadventure, then pushed on toward Fort Reno, at the edge of the Badlands. He had almost reached it when the Indians struck. It was a minor attack, and when the braves felt the unexpected power and rapid fire from the Remington breechloaders, they withdrew to think things over and wonder what to do next. Story pushed on, but one cowboy had been killed and two others were wounded. His effective strength had been reduced ten per cent, but there were no incidents between Fort Reno and Fort Kearney, the Army's farthest outpost in Indian territory.

For a few days it was a quiet trip, the cattle browsing as they moved. Then, one sunny autumn afternoon, the first test came. Crazy Horse and his band attacked. There were hordes of Indians—some reports say there were 500 of them. Letting the cattle fend for themselves, the cowboys formed their wagons in a circle and waited. In traditional fashion, the warriors dashed up close enough to draw the little band's fire. Then they waited for the lull that would indicate the men were reloading before they made a serious charge. The Indians were used to facing muzzle-loaders, and there had always been such a lull. But not this day. The rapid firing Remingtons enabled the cowboys to keep up a steady, galling fire that had braves dropping from their horses at an alarming rate. The Sioux retired to lick their wounds and to fight another day. Two other days, it developed, for there were three attacks in all before the Indians gave up without tak-

An emigrant wagon train attacked by hostile Indians

69

The Paris International Exhibition, 1867; many Remington guns were on display. Shown is the pavilion of the Emperor of Paris

ing a single scalp. Twenty-seven men had stood off odds of almost twenty to one, and they had succeeded in driving their cattle through to Montana. The Remington rolling block had proved its worth in a spectacular fashion.

It kept right on proving it, in both America and Europe. At the Imperial Exposition of 1867, in Paris, the Remington was unanimously selected by the High Commission on Firearms as "the finest rifle in the world." It was awarded the Silver Medal of the Exposition, the highest award for military and sporting arms. Even more impressive was the response of military boards throughout the world. Denmark adopted the rolling block as an official arm that same year. Norway and Sweden followed in 1868, Spain in 1869, Egypt in 1870, and Argentina in 1879. Several other South American countries, as well as China, Austria, and Italy also purchased the Remington rolling

70

Headquarters Fort Abraham Lincoln, D. T.
October 5, 1873.

MESSRS. REMINGTON & SONS:

Dear Sirs—Last year I ordered from your firm a Sporting Rifle, caliber .50. I received the rifle a short time prior to the departure of the Yellowstone Expedition. The Expedition left Fort Rice the 20th of June, 1873, and returned to Fort Abraham Lincoln, September 21, 1873. During the period of three months I carried the rifle referred to on every occasion and the following list exhibits but a portion of the game killed by me: Antelope 41; buffalo 4; elk 4; blacktail deer 4; American deer 3; white wolf 2; geese, prairie chickens and other feathered game in large numbers.

The number of animals killed is not so remarkable as the distance at which the shots were executed. The average distance at which the forty-one antelopes were killed was 250 yards by actual measurement. I rarely obtained a shot at an antelope under 150 yards, while the range extended from that distance up to 630 yards.

With the expedition were professional hunters employed by the Government to obtain game for the troops. Many of the officers and men also were excellent shots, and participated extensively in hunting along the line of march. I was the only person who used one of your Rifles, which, as may properly be stated, there were pitted against it breech-loading rifles of almost every description, including many of the Springfield breechloaders altered to Sporting Rifles. With your Rifle I killed far more game than any other single party, professional or amateur, while the shots made with your rifle were at longer range and more difficult shots than were those made by any other rifles in the command. I am more than ever impressed with the many superior qualities possessed by the system of arms manufactured by your firm, and I believe I am safe in asserting that to a great extent this opinion is largely shared by the members of the Yellowstone Expedition who had the opportunity to make practical tests of the question.

I am truly yours,
G. A. Custer
BREVET MAJOR GENERAL U.S. ARMY

A tired General George Custer of the U.S. Cavalry

block in some quantities, and almost every nation experimented with it. In all, more than a million rolling block military rifles and carbines were manufactured and sold, including 33,000 manufactured at the Springfield Armory for use of the Army and Navy.

But the rolling block was by no means a military arm only. Thousands and thousands were made as sporting rifles, and they were welcomed by the nation's hunters and target shooters. One of the most delighted was George Armstrong Custer. A western hunter of great experience, Custer was also a gun enthusiast, and his quarters in the various posts where he was stationed always held racks of pistols, rifles and shotguns. When the rolling block reached the market, he was quick to order a specially engraved model. After using it a year, he wrote the company an unsolicited testimonial relating his exploits with the rifle. Few other people could speak from such personal experience!

To the end, Custer remained enthusiastic about his Remington, taking it with him on all important hunts and military expeditions. It was with him in his last battle, but no rifle could have saved him from the hordes of Sioux at the Little Big Horn. There were just too many Indians. One of them rode off with Custer's fine Remington. No one ever reported seeing it again.

Pistols, too, were made with the rolling block action—some military, some civilian. Both the Army and Navy ordered rolling block

On the 25th of June at Little Big Horn, General George Custer, his brothers, his nephew and 5 troops of cavalry were killed

pistols, the Navy in 1866 and 1867, the Army in 1871. More than 12,000 in all were purchased by the United States Government. For the civilian, however, the rolling block pistol offered a superb target arm. Not only did it provide strong simple breech action, but its balance and holding qualities were excellent.

What other action has ever been acclaimed with such world-wide success and continued in use for so long a period? The catalytic action of outstanding designers working at Remington had produced a true masterpiece, a classic of firearms design.

73

CHAPTER SIX

FOR SCHUETZENFESTS AND "BELLY-WHOMPERS"

Most target matches were serious
occasions, but Schuetzenfests
brimmed over with gemütlichkeit

FOR SCHUETZENFESTS AND "BELLYWHOMPERS"

Target shooting is an American tradition. Almost as soon as the colonists set foot on American shores, they began to vie with each other in shooting at marks. It is true that there are no records of formal competitive matches in the Jamestown colony of 1607, but the Pilgrims of Plymouth are known to have amazed Indians by potting crows in flight as a test of skill. Other early colonies also witnessed competition with firearms, especially after the German settlers brought the rifle to this country. Members of rifle regiments enlisting for the American Revolution were sometimes selected on the basis of marksmanship competitions, and Washington even ordered prizes for the best shots with the smoothbore muskets in his regular infantry regiments.

In 1871, the National Rifle Association of America was formed to guide the marksmen of the young nation—and almost immediately it received a challenge from abroad that led it into international competition as well.

This first challenge came from Ireland. In 1873, an Irish rifle team had defeated the best marksmen of England and Scotland in a national match at Wimbledon. They had won one of the most important shooting contests in the world, and it seemed to make them rifle champions of the English-speaking world. But did it? There were still the Americans, who

☞ *Preceding page, top to bottom: rifles—Remington International Free, Hepburn target, rolling block, Remington-Schuetzen Match, No. 5 rolling block*

had a reputation for being rifle shots because of their military exploits. True, the Americans didn't even have a national competition of their own. They were rank amateurs, but the Irish could not rest content until they had proved their superiority over any one and everyone who might possibly have a claim to competence with a rifle. They sent a challenge in the form of a newspaper advertisement addressed simply to "The Riflemen of the United States". (They didn't even know there was a national association.) The National Rifle Association was a bit miffed that it had been overlooked, but it had competitors with enough pride not to let this stand in the way. This question of national supremacy with the rifle had to be settled. Through the device of the "Amateur Rifle Association" they accepted the gauntlet and immediately began to hold elimination contests to determine who should represent the United States in the competition. First, however, came the question of raising funds to match the prize money that the Irish had suggested be put up, and second came the matter of selecting proper rifles. There was no such thing as an American long range target rifle readily available.

A Schuetzenfest shooting gallery at Jones's Wood

This is where E. Remington & Sons stepped into the picture. The Remington brothers not only offered to design some special target rifles for half of the selected American team, but they also put up a sizeable portion of the money that would match the Irish challenge funds. The Sharps Rifle Company was equally

77

The California Sensation!!

DR. W. F. CARVER,
OF CALIFORNIA.
THE CHAMPION RIFLE SHOT OF THE WORLD

Those who were good enough could make a handsome living from shooting. Carver sold a half interest in his shows for $25,000

prepared, and they supplied the other rifles and the rest of the necessary money. Thanks to the N. R. A. and the two companies, America was ready to accept the challenge.

Negotiations and arrangements followed. September 26, 1874, was selected as the date.

Fanned by articles in the New York *Herald,* feeling ran high. The Irish had stipulated that only American-born marksmen could compete against them, so this was to be truly a test of American skill with the national weapon. It

78

A seaside shooting gallery. This gallery closely resembles those of today at coastal resort areas

would be highly embarrassing to lose. What would happen to America's reputation as a nation of riflemen? Yet the Irish were highly skilled shots. They had beaten the best marksmen of western Europe with an astonishing score, while the Americans, who were used to shooting at much shorter ranges, had not even had a first class long-distance range until Creedmoor had been built two years before. It had no practiced national team. Instead, it had merely announced a competition for places and selected the team from the best shots who entered. It would be a contest of rookies against highly skilled marksmen.

Shooting at plaster casts to display expert marksmanship

In rifles, however, the American team more than held its own. The Irish used fine rifles made by John Rigby of Dublin, himself a member of the rifle team. They were muzzle-loaders. Both the Sharps and Remington companies, however, decided to produce breechloaders, despite the contention of many conservatives that only muzzle-loading rifles could offer the accuracy necessary for long-range shooting. The Remington brothers assigned

79

the task of designing their rifle to Lewis L. Hepburn, superintendent of their mechanical department and also one of the successful competitors for a place on the American team. Hepburn selected the famous rolling block action. Then he designed a beautiful firearm around it, with adjustable Vernier and wind-gauge sights, a pistol-grip stock and wonderful holding qualities. It was an arm to catch the eye of any rifleman and, after its sterling performance in the competition, it was manufactured commercially as the Remington-Creedmoor rifle.

For months, the American team practiced with their new rifles. Then September 26 dawned clear and hot. Thousands of spectators crowded against the guard ropes at Creedmoor to watch the shooting, and they were not disappointed. They were treated to some excellent marksmanship—and some magnificent acrobatics, as the American and Irish shooters adopted the positions they liked best. The majority lay prone in a version of the traditional position, but others lay on their backs with their legs crossed and still others lay half on their backs and half on their sides, all in an effort for a steadier position and firmer control of their rifles. At such long ranges, the slightest deviation could mean a complete miss.

The first contest was at 800 yards, and the Americans won by a score of 326 to 317. There was no real rejoicing, however, for the Americans were expected to do their best at the shortest range, less well at longer ranges.

Turkey shooting was a favorite pastime, especially during the holidays. Hitting a moving turkey proved to be a difficult shot

At 900 yards, the Irish pulled ahead by a tiny margin, 312 to 310. But an unsual thing had happened. J. K. Milner, one of the best shots on the Irish team, had hit the wrong target! He was one of those shooters who fired while lying on his back with the rifle barrel resting between his feet. In this position, his field of vision was narrowed to what he could see in the V formed by his toes. Somehow, in lying down, he had lined his feet up with the target in the next lane, and his bull's-eye counted for nothing but a wasted shot.

At 1,000 yards, the Irish again pulled ahead 302 to 298, but it was not enough, and the Americans won a surprising victory 934 to 931. Had Milner not aimed at the wrong target, however, the story would have been different and Ireland would have won by a single point. That was how close it was. The United States

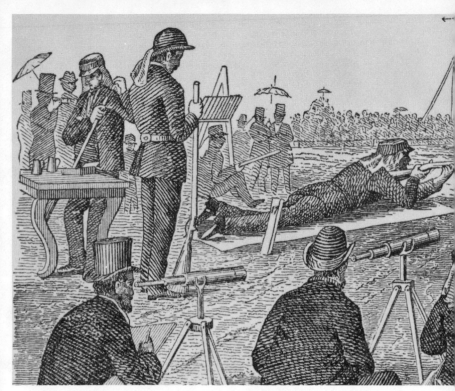

American rifle team was challenged by the world famous Irish team and

could rejoice in its victory, but the Irish team could solace itself with the knowledge that they had really shot better—if only the errant bull had been on the right target!

The outcome of the match might not have been really decisive, but the performance of the rifles certainly was. America now had two long-distance target rifles that could rank with the best in the world. Remington was especially happy, for Henry Fulton, who had fired the best American score—and one of the best in the whole competition—had used a Remington. To confound the experts, however, he had used it as a breech-muzzle-loader. That is, he had inserted the cartridge with its powder charge through the breech, but had

the two met at Creedmoor, Long Island, where America won the match

patched and loaded the bullet from the muzzle. Many conservative shooters did this in the later years of the 1800's, until they finally became convinced that a breechloader with factory ammunition could be just as accurate as the most carefully patched ball loaded from the muzzle.

For years, the Remington-Creedmoor rifle was a popular item in the catalog, and it was soon joined by other fine target rifles. The mid range and short range rifles were generally similar, but lacked the precision sights of the long range Creedmoor. Then, in 1880, Lewis Hepburn produced a new action. It is hard to conceive of any action being better than the rolling block, but the Hepburn was certainly

83

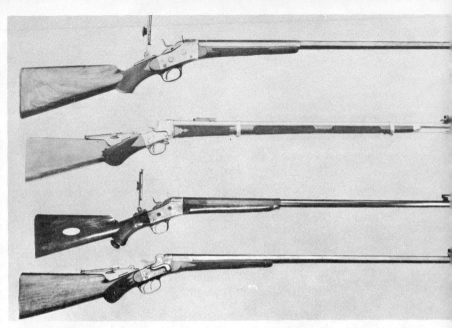

Top to bottom: Remington mid-range rolling block, Hepburn No. 3, Remington Creedmoor, No. 3 Improved Creedmoor Hepburn

a good one, and it appealed to many shooters. It consisted of a falling block that moved vertically in a mortise when it was activated by a finger lever on the right side of the breech. It was a smoother looking action than the rolling block, and it required fewer movements to operate it. Remington featured it on its No. 3 Improved Creedmoor rifle from 1880 until 1907.

With these fine rifles, Remington had taken good care of the lie-down shooters, but there were other marksmen who also wanted target rifles. These were the offhand shooters, especially the members of the various Schuetzen clubs scattered throughout the country. Schuetzen competitions were as old as shooting itself. They were offhand matches, shot without any support but the muscles of the marksman himself. They required both a

84

Marksmen made positions famous. From top to bottom: Henry Fulton, G. W. Yale, John Bodine

sturdy body and keen eyesight, for they were frequently fired at ranges of 200 yards. At that distance, the only shots that counted were those that struck squarely in the six-inch bull's-eye. No wonder the Schuetzen fraternity looked with scorn on the "belly-whompers"!

The first Schuetzen matches were held in Germany and Switzerland in the fifteenth century, and they were popular throughout all of central Europe. When colonists from this area came to America in the early 1700's they brought their love of shooting with them, but the rigid rules of the European contests were soon modified on the frontier. Then new immigrants in the middle of the nineteenth century brought the formal contests to America once again. This time they remained pure —and they became immensely popular. By 1866, the first national Schuetzenfest was held

Half-stocked No. 3 Remington-Hepburn, the new version

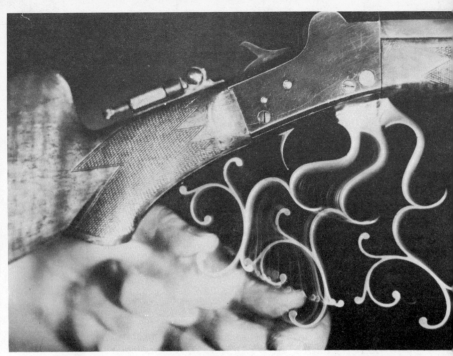

Remington-Schuetzen rifle. Modification of standard Remington-Hepburn action, using an under lever, sliding breechblock

in New York City, and following years saw more and more regional and national meets.

No one who has seen a Schuetzen match could ever forget it. What a contrast to the slow and deadly serious firing of the lie-down marksmen and their silent audience! At the Schuetzen matches there were food, song, jollity and *gemütlichkeit*. Crowds came for the sociability. On the firing line, the shooters were just as serious—but in a different way. Each man would stand holding his heavy rifle and peering at the distant targets. Sometimes he would stand swaying slightly for five or more minutes, then lay the rifle down and walk back to the refreshment table for a foaming stein of beer. Draining the mug, he would take his place on the line once again, patiently

86

Schuetzen with peep sight, in a choice of four calibers

The Schuetzen stand was a site of hearty drinking

holding his heavy rifle until he was satisfied with his aim. Then he would pull the trigger.

Schuetzen rifles were abnormally heavy guns, weighing up to sixteen pounds. But most important of all was the shape of their butts. The butt plate itself was broad, with two long arms projecting at the top and bottom. These prongs passed over and under the arm of the shooter and gave him better control of his piece. An added feature on some rifles was a folding palm rest for the left hand, attached to the forearm.

Remington began to make Schuetzen rifles in the late 1800's, and they continued until that fascinating sport disappeared at the beginning of World War I. Both the rolling block and the Hepburn action were offered with the pronged buttplate, and the palm rest could be had, too, if it was wanted. The Schuetzen rifles were both beautiful and highly unusual.

87

CHAPTER SEVEN

RIDING SHOTGUN

Single barrel, double barrel, over-and-under—shotguns helped push the frontier toward the coast

RIDING SHOTGUN

Few other firearms can do all the things a shotgun can, and few have had so long and colorful a history. After all, the shotgun was the very first specialized sporting arm to appear back in the early 1600's, and it has been in continuous use ever since. Loaded with shot pellets, it has been used to bag fowl of all sorts as well as small game. Loaded with a single slug, it has brought down deer and buffalo, even bear and wild boar.

Remington recognized the importance of the shotgun from the very beginning. Some of the first guns that Lite made were single-barreled models. He also made double-barreled sporting guns with one rifled barrel and one shotgun barrel, so that the hunter or perhaps the Forty-niner could have his choice of the most efficient firearm for the task at hand. These were muzzle-loading arms, first in flintlock and then percussion. When the famous rolling block system appeared in 1866, it was promptly applied to shotguns as well as rifles and pistols.

The progression from muzzle-loading, percussion-lock shotguns to modern breech-loading doubles, pumps, and autoloaders was greatly enhanced by two developments. The first was the perfection of paper and brass center fire shotgun shells and the second was the invention of choke boring.

 Preceding page, left to right: shotguns—model 870 pump action; double-barrel Remington-Whittmore; model 1100 autoloader; and model 1894 hammerless

The first practical center fire breech-loading shotgun shells made their appearance in the middle of the last century, at about the same time as their rifle and pistol counterparts. Initially, these shells were made with all brass cases and center fire primers, and they were generally sold unloaded. Shooters added their own powder, wads and shot to their own specifications. By the early 1870's, a far less expensive shell, utilizing a brass head and a tightly wound paper body, had been developed. Marcellus Hartley, the founder of the Union Metallic Cartridge Company, the predecessor of Remington's ammunition business—he was later to become the owner of Remington Arms —felt there was a market for factory loaded paper and brass shotgun shells. His new product, introduced in the mid-70's, met with almost instant success and was a large factor in the growth of his ammunition business.

Shooting at ducks off the lake at Saratoga, New York

The exact origins of choke boring are obscure. Various types and styles of bore constriction had been tried in European fowling pieces at least from the closing of the eighteenth century. But it was W. R. Pape of England, and J. W. Long and Fred Kimble of the United States, who brought the idea forcibly to the attention of the sportsmen of the English-speaking world in the years after the American Civil War. A common shotgun of the period, with a uniform bore diameter from breech to muzzle, did well to place 40 per cent of its shot in a 30-inch circle at 40 yards. With a constricted bore near the muzzle, as advo-

91

cated by Long and Kimble, the shot charge held together for a longer period after leaving the bore, and the effective range of the gun was increased considerably. Remington and other manufacturers were quick to adopt the idea. Today, a wide variety of chokes is available, ranging from "open cylinder" (none at all for short range) to "modified" (about half choke for medium range) to "full" (for long range).

Strange as it may seem, however, it was not until 1873 that Remington brought out its first true double-barreled shotgun. When it did appear, the model 1873 was an important firearm. Previously, the great majority of double guns had been imported from Europe—and good ones had carried a high price tag. Remington's new model was a fine gun at a moderate price, right in line with the company's long-standing goal. It was a breechloader with the break-open breech that is familiar to most shooters as the oldest of all breech-loading shotgun actions. It opened with a top lever that had to be pushed up by the thumb, and this was a bit awkward. A new version appeared in 1882, with the side-moving top lever that is still common in doubles today. Small game hunters and wildfowlers quickly took to the Remington doubles, and the great Wells Fargo Express thought so well of them that they purchased a quantity of the Remington shotguns for their stage guards to use in protecting the valuable cargoes going to and from the fast-growing western cities.

With the invention of shotguns, bird shooting became popular. An illustration by Major shows American teal hunting in 1858

By this time, there was also a demand for double shotguns from a rapidly developing new group of trap shooters. The whole idea of competitive shooting at bird targets had been developed in England in the early nineteenth century, and by 1831 it had crossed to America. At first, live pigeons had simply been placed under the top hats of the period. At the command "pull" from the shooter, an attendant yanked a string that tipped over the hat and released the bird, which promptly took off in whatever direction it happened to be pointed at the time. Later, collapsible traps replaced the big hats. Trap shooting with live birds was a real test of skill for the shooter, but it was not a scientific test. A new target appeared in the form of the artificial pigeon. Glass balls came first, in 1866. They were hurled by a spring-actuated trap, and

93

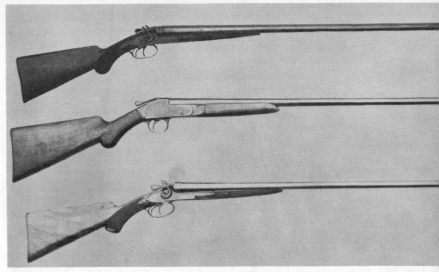

Top to bottom: model 89, double barrel; Remington-Rider No. 3 shotgun, single barrel; New Model 1882, double barrel shotgun

some of the earliest ones were filled with feathers so the successful shot could actually "see the feathers fly." Next came the clay pigeon, invented by George Ligowski about 1879, and quickly improved by Fred Kimble to bring it to its modern form.

The first Grand American Handicap Trapshoot was held at Dexter Park, New York, in 1893. It was highly successful, and national championships quickly came to be annual events. Live birds were still used at first, but in 1900 both live targets and clay pigeons were used, as a gradual shift toward a more scientific (and humane) competition. This idea found quick appeal, and since 1902 only clay pigeons have been used.

Trapshooting has continued to grow in favor, and today its popularity is at an all-time high. In essence, the game has changed little since the turn of the century—although there have been vast improvements in ammunition and shotguns. There are three main events in

94

Trap shooting became so popular that it was deemed fashionable for women to compete. Here, a lady was the eventual winner

registered competition: 16 yard, handicap, and doubles. In 16 yard shooting, a squad of five shooters lines up abreast in a semicircle 16 yards in back of a low shed, which houses the trap. Targets are thrown at constant vertical angles and varying horizontal angles, all going away from the shooter. Shooters fire in turn at five targets from each station. Thus one "round" consists of 25 targets. Additional shooting stations are located on paths extending back from the 16 yard posts at intervals from one yard to 27 yards behind the trap house. In handicap shooting, competitors shoot from varying yardages, based on known ability from past performance. In doubles, two targets are thrown from the trap simultaneously on different angles. Shooters, for this event, are stationed on the 16 yard positions.

In the early 1920's, a new clay target game, later christened "skeet," came into popularity. A group of New England sportsmen devised this new sport in an attempt to create a shot-

95

At one time, woods were overflowing with game and fish

gun shooting game that more closely simulated conditions found in upland hunting. Instead of shooting only at targets going away at varying angles, as in trap, they set up shooting stations on a semicircle between two traps. The shooters move around the semicircle, shooting from eight positions at birds thrown at constant angles from each of the two traps.

In the early days of trap and skeet shooting, the shotguns used were generally no different from those employed for hunting. As the sports developed and became more stylized, however, the demand for specialized models became apparent. Remington met it.

The hammerless models of 1894 and the model 1900, both double-barreled arms, were made with full choke barrels and special stock dimensions for trap shooting. Single-barreled trap models were also offered and, in 1907, the first of the slide or pump action repeaters, which have been popular ever since, was introduced. This gun and later modifications were based on a design patented in 1905 by John D. Pedersen, who assigned his patent to Remington. Here again, it was a case of the company setting out to acquire a fine action, obtaining it, and producing a great gun to go with it. The slide action was, of course, made in field grades for hunting, as well as in trap grades.

After skeet became popular in the 1920's, specialized guns for it were also developed. These shotguns featured standard field grade stock dimensions with short barrels fitted with ventilated ribs and special open chokes.

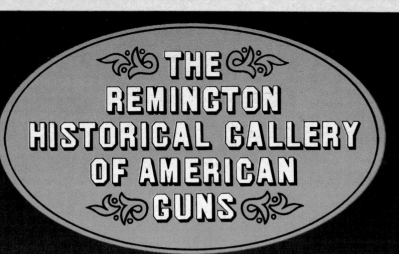

THE REMINGTON HISTORICAL GALLERY OF AMERICAN GUNS

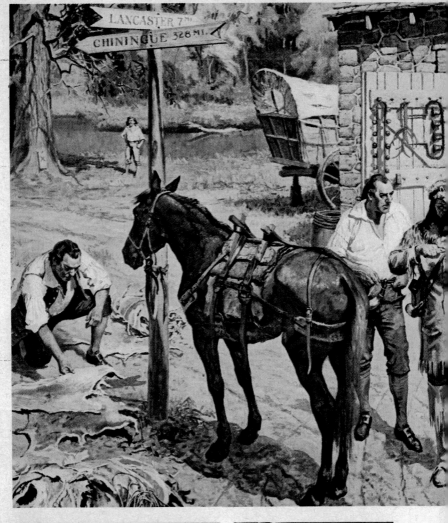

PHLF 86

Ever since the discovery of the formula for gunpowder, men have been trying to make better firearms. The first of the American colonists had good reason to want better guns, ones that would be equal to the challenge of the wilderness. They had only the awkward matchlock with which to conquer the woods and its inhabitants. The chances of hitting anything smaller than a grapefruit at more than 20 paces with a matchlock were slim, and setting one off was a time-consuming chore. First the powder had to be poured down the barrel and then the ball hammered in after it. A bit more powder was sprinkled into the priming pan and a lighted wick used to fire it. By the time young Eliphalet Remington of New York state learned to shoot, the flintlock was the standard firearm. "Lite" Remington determined to turn out a better precision-built rifle of his own design, using his own tools. In a short time he succeeded. Drawings—above: typical Pennsylvania gun factory, which made the flintlock of the times; left, Eliphalet Remington bronze sculpture and view of his forge.

Although it had its drawbacks, the flintlock proved to be a much more efficient rifle than its predecessors, the wheelock and the matchlock. In the flintlock, a piece of flint was held in a clamp on the end of a pivoted arm called a cock. Opposite it was a piece of steel fastened to the lid of a pan that the shooter filled with gunpowder before each shot. Pulling the trigger released the cock, which sprang forward to strike steel, sending a shower of sparks for ignition and also opening the lid of the pan to expose the powder. The resulting flash passed through a hole in the side of the barrel to set off the main charge inside. Left: the first Remington—a muzzle-loading flintlock; breech-loading Jenks with a Maynard-tape lock; combination percussion-lock rifle and shotgun; muzzle-loading percussion lock "Zouave"; center fire No. 1 rolling block rifle; center fire .43 caliber rolling block rifle; the New Model Army revolver; over and under derringer.

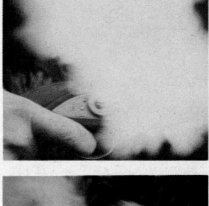

Back in the days of Eliphalet Remington, making a rifle barrel was a long and tedious job. First, a long strip of soft metal was chosen and forge-heated until red hot. The strip of metal was wrapped around a rod to form the bore, and then welded under a hammer with a flux of borax and sand to make the joint stick. For work on the outside of the barrel, Eliphalet used a water-driven grindstone and a file to dress it down and form the flat faces of the much-admired octagonal form. In later years, the octagonal form was achieved by forging, but the early precision of hand filing was difficult to match. Completing the inside of the bore was an equally tedious job, and could only ▮ done with special equipment. Reami▮ came first, to smooth out the rou▮ interior. Then came rifling—groovi▮ the interior so that the bullet would ta▮ on spin as it left the barrel and th▮ maintain a straight direction. The futu▮ would bring special steel equipmer▮ but for Eliphalet, rifling was done ▮ means of a hickory rod. A small cutti▮ tooth on the end of the rod cut ea▮ groove as it was pushed back and for▮ through the bore with a pre-set twisti▮ motion controlled by an indexing guic▮ When all the scratching was finished, ▮ paper-thin shim was put under t▮ tooth to make it protrude farther, a▮

e process was begun again. As the
rrel now stood, it was just a simple,
ed tube, open at both ends. Further
rk was needed to forge a plug for it,
d cut threads so that it could be
rewed into the breech end of the bar-
as a means of closing it. The breech
ig also would hold the tang used to
sten the barrel to the stock. When the
rrel was all finished and sights had
en added, Eliphalet browned it, prob-
ly with a mixture of urine and iron
ide, to reduce glare when sighting
d also to help prevent any rust. The
quence photos on these pages show
rrel rifling with steel equipment, forg-
g for barrel shape, and rifling tools.

Guns had been in existence long before the first settlers came to America, but the more delicate European arms were no match for the wilderness of the new country. Yet, as the frontier spread westward away from the Atlantic Coast colonies, there evolved a gun uniquely American. This was the long—or Kentucky—rifle, the first precision rifle ever made. The Kentucky had two vitally important features. The first was its much smaller bore—.50 caliber or less, which meant that a frontiersman could comfortably carry enough bullets with him for long treks across virgin lands. The second vital feature was the very long barrel, which allowed a minimum charge of powder to burn completely, using all its power before the bullet left the muzzle. Thus, powder, too, was con-

served. The barrel had another advantage: it was extremely heavy, muffling the report so that the direction from which the shot came could not easily be detected by any hostile Indians nearby. The rifle was a quick one to load because the ball was a bit undersized. It was enveloped in a simple greased patch and rammed home in one stroke. The kick of the powder charge then expanded it enough to fill the grooves of the rifling. The Kentucky rifle, in short, was sturdy and supremely accurate, with a shooting record unmatched anywhere in the world. Armed with this, Daniel Boone was able to explore and help colonize Kentucky. Illustrated at the left are percussion lock half-stocked rifles which had evolved from the original flintlock rifle called "Kentucky."

By 1847, Remington gunsmiths had learned to drill steel, producing a far harder and more accurate barrel than the iron barrels of the earlier flintlocks. The new method was put to use on a new rifle—a breechloader called the Jenks carbine, created by a gunsmith named William Jenks. Although loading from the breech was not a new idea, the Jenks was one of the first practical adaptations of it. When the breech was opened, the powder and ball were loaded from the rear. Powder was then sprinkled lightly over the ball. With the gun loaded, the breech was locked tight. The ignition system was new, too. Instead of priming powder, caps that were exploded by a simple blow were used—sending sparks straight to the powder charge. In the Jenks carbine, these percussion caps were arranged on a tape, as in a cap pistol; a new one moved into place with each shot. The Jenks system was simple and fast, capable of a rapid fire that brought something new to the gun world. In 1847, when the Mexican War began in earnest, the U.S. Marines had the carbines in hand. The far superior fire-power of American soldiers decimated a numerically superior Mexican army, and the Marines and Army stormed through Vera Cruz and on to Mexico City, where they assaulted the great fortress of Chapultepec. The Jenks carbine also was used in successful cattle drives like the one shown on opposite page in lithograph of Russells' "The Wagon Boss."

The growth of cities and the expansion west brought a need for a new kind of defense weapon—a small gun that could be carried easily and concealed when necessary. Just such a gun was invented by Sam Colt, and it was aptly named the revolver. In the time it took for the Colt patent to expire, Remington had designed a new revolver. Teaming with Fordyce Beals, Remington came out with his first pocket weapon—the Remington-Beals. The gun was light, weighing only 11 ounces. It fired a .31 caliber ball and offered five shots ready for instant use. It came complete with brass bullet mold, copper powder flask, and brass bullet seater. Beals made improvements, adding an inch to the barrel length and adding a loading lever, so that the separate and easily lost bullet seater was no longer needed. At 14 ounces, the gun was still a light one. For the horseman to carry in a holster, Beals invented a new type of loading lever and cylinder pin and incorporated them into larger revolvers called the Beals Army and Beals Navy. From these two guns came the Remington New Model, perhaps the finest percussion revolver made. Remington then went to smaller guns, starting with a .17 caliber percussion cap pistol designed by

oseph Rider, ending with William H. lliot's famous double derringer. Remngton ended up producing thousands f defense weapons, both revolvers and ocket pistols alike, for the homeowner, torekeeper, traveler, and even for men uch as General George Custer. Left and page: "Custer's Last Stand." ight hand page, top: typical western aloon. Center, left: remodeled 1890 nd 1875 Army revolvers; right: single-ction, new line revolver; four-barreled, ouble-action, Elliot revolver; Elliot's ouble derringer; Iroquois single-acon, .22 caliber revolver. Bottom: 860-88 percussion A & N revolvers.

e invention of the breechloader led
 the development of the finest single-
ot rifle of its time—the Remington
lling block. The shooter first cocked
e hammer; then, with his thumb, he
led back the breechblock and ex-
sed the opening into the bore. If he
d already fired a shot, this action also
tracted the spent cartridge case. In
s position the new load was inserted,
e shooter rolled the breechblock back
o place, and the gun was ready to
e. Furthermore, instead of a paper
rtridge, a metallic cartridge was
ed, keeping intact all the bullet's
wer. Above: buffalo being shot with
 rifle of the time. Bottom right: the
lling block mechanism. Left: rolling
ck carbine; the Merrill Sporting rifle;
aynard-tape lock musket; the Reming-
n "Zouave"; and the Jenks carbine.

The Wild West was beginning to b
tame. Civilized towns sprang up at a
amazing rate; the Indians had bee
subdued, and wars finally appeared t
be over. The glory and romance of th
Old West was brought east, and peop
came by the thousands to get a glimps
of Buffalo Bill and Sitting Bull—an
Annie Oakley. With a lightweight 2(
gauge shotgun for flying targets or wit
one of the new Remington .22 calib
automatics, she could center drill ar
target in sight. Annie Oakley was th
forerunner of the name of the gam
today—sport shooting. Thousands
people turned to rifles as a new for
of sport. Trap, skeet, and target shoo
ing, as well as hunting grouse and oth
game, became immensely popular. Ar
so, finally able to return to its origin
intentions, Remington now produc
thousands of sporting rifles—rifles bo
of guns that tamed the wildernes

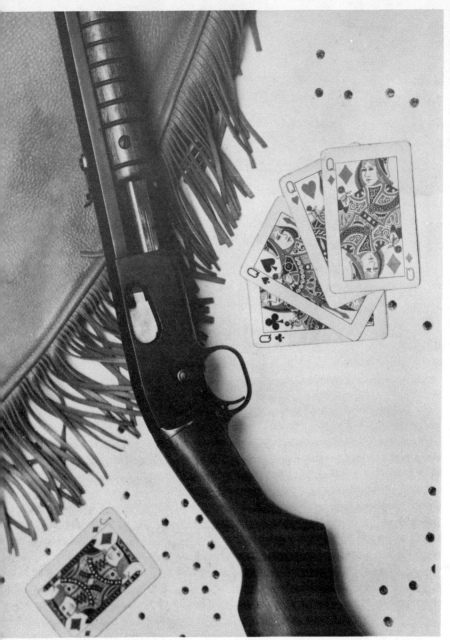

*The gun that Annie Oakley used—a Remington model 12, 10 shot
to 15 shot according to size of cartridge. Slide action repeating
rifle. Steel barrel. Calibers .22 short, long and long rifle*

CHAPTER EIGHT

THE BANJO-PLAYING BROWNING BROTHERS

John was the inventor, Matthew
the businessman—and both
were superb American gunsmiths

THE BANJO-PLAYING BROWNING BROTHERS

The Remington company that manufactured the Pedersen slide-action shotgun and its associated models in 1907 was a far different organization from the one which had brought out the first Remington double-barreled shotgun in 1874. For one thing, there were no longer any Remingtons in the company. Sam had died in 1882 and, without his salesmanship and business acumen, the company had slid deep into financial difficulty, despite a strong continuing demand for Remington guns. Finally, it had become too much for the remaining brothers, and they declared themselves bankrupt.

Interestingly enough, the firm was not really in as bad shape as the financial records indicate. All it needed was a good businessman to take charge and revitalize it. That man quickly appeared—Marcellus Hartley, a partner in the famous sporting and military goods firm of Schuyler, Hartley & Graham of New York City, and a founder of the Union Metallic Cartridge Company of Bridgeport, Connecticut. By 1888, Hartley was in complete charge of Remington. The sales force was combined with that of the Union Metallic Cartridge Company, to obtain maximum exposure for both. Other than that, there were few changes. The tradition and quality of the Remington operation were maintained. Even the name re-

---

Preceding page,   left to right: the model 8 autoloading rifle; the "Sportsman" model 11 autoloading; model 1100 autoloading shotguns

mained, changing simply from E. Remington & Sons to the Remington Arms Company.

Hartley ran the Remington firm well. Under his guidance, it regained its financial solidity while retaining its high standards of workmanship and its constant search for better arms. Then, in 1902, Hartley collapsed at a board meeting and died.

By an ironic coincidence, even Hartley's death was linked to the furtherance of the Remington tradition. When he died, two men were waiting in his anteroom to show him the models of two new guns. One held an autoloading shotgun, the other an autoloading sporting rifle. Their names were John and Matthew Browning.

Marcellus Hartley, an early moving force at Remington

The Brownings were not newcomers to the field of gun design. John had already designed highly successful arms for Colt and Winchester, but they now felt John had developed perhaps his most important breakthrough in firearms design in these recoil operated sporting guns. They knew of Remington's interest in improved arms, and they knew of the Remington reputation for quality arms and for fine relations with designers and workmen. The Brownings would have been welcome anywhere, but they had chosen Remington.

Hartley's sudden death at first threw their plans into confusion. However, Marcellus Hartley Dodge, who succeeded his grandfather as president, jumped at the chance to manufacture the Browning-designed arms on a royalty basis, and the Browning brothers went to

117

First factory of Browning Brothers. Remington and Browning teamed to produce many firearms

work in the plant, setting up the machinery for manufacturing their new guns. Salty individuals to the bone, they amazed the other workmen by the sulphurous content of their arguments, and entertained them with banjo renditions of popular songs when work was over. John was the inventor, Matthew the businessman, but both were good mechanics. By late 1905, the first examples of the model 11 autoloading shotgun were rolling off the workbenches, and the model 8 autoloading rifle quickly followed. With these two guns, Remington became the first manufacturer in America to offer autoloading arms to the sporting public.

These were fast-firing firearms. Both had a five shot capacity, the rifle boasting a box magazine and the shotgun a tubular magazine under the barrel. In the shotgun action that John

19th century illustrations of frontier life frequently made the point that a powerful rifle was the only defense against bears

Browning had devised, the bolt was held in its closed position by a spring and toggle arrangement. When the gun was fired, the shot charge was propelled from the muzzle by the force of expanding powder gases in the conventional manner. The recoil effect, created by this, pushed the bolt and the barrel, which were locked together, all the way to the rear. When the bolt had gone as far back as it could, it unlocked from the barrel and was held back for a moment, while the barrel was carried forward by a spring in the fore-end. When the barrel reached its firing position, it hit a latch that released the bolt. The spring behind the bolt then carried it forward, a new shell was fed up from the magazine, and the gun locked up, ready for the next shot. The rifle action differed from that of the shotgun in that the breech was closed by a set of double lugs on

119

Top to bottom: model 742 autoloading rifle; the "Sportsman" 58 shotgun; 1931-1948 model 11 shotgun; model 8 autoloading rifle

a turning bolt that locked the cartridge firmly in position until the projectile had left the barrel. The barrel recoiled inside a jacket while locked to the bolt.

Experienced hunters knew that sometimes the availability of quick shots could mean the difference between life and death to a hunter. Take, for instance, the adventure of "Big Bill" Hillis of Alaska. One day Bill and a companion named King went bear hunting on Kodiak Island. They were inching their way along a narrow ledge on a sheer cliff when they suddenly found a family of five bears right in their path. This was a good deal more than they cared to tackle, but they could not retreat fast enough to get away from the bears, who very apparently were in an ugly mood. As the lead bear (who turned out to be a big male) reared up, Bill leveled his Remington autoloader and fired. It was a clean hit, and the huge animal dropped in his tracks. Meanwhile, King had fallen down and let fly with his own rifle at the mother bear, who was immediately behind the male. Since he had to fire between Bill's legs, his aim was not the best; he succeeded only in wounding the animal. Enraged, the beast charged, with the three large youngsters right behind. It was a tight situation in every sense of the word, but Bill was equal to it. With four quick shots he killed all four of the remaining bears before they could reach him. It was tremendous shooting, but if Bill hadn't had a rifle as fast and as powerful as the Remington autoloader, he could not possibly have done it.

There were other shooters who admired the rapidity of the autoloaders. These were the professional marksmen and trick shooters who made speed a part of their demonstrations. For many years, Remington maintained champion shooters and teams of marksmen with rifle and shotgun to publicize the quality of their arms and ammunition. One trick shot who became a Remington salesman was Frank Butler. He was a highly skilled performer with all sorts of firearms, but his wife was even better. Her name was Annie Oakley. Frank had first met Annie when they competed in a shooting match, and he fell in love with her while she set about beating him by one point.

121

BUFFALO BILL'S WILD WEST
AND CONGRESS OF ROUGH RIDERS OF THE WORLD.

WILD RIVALRIES OF SAVAGE, BARBAROUS AND CIVILIZED RACES.

Flamboyant posters like this advertising the appearance of Buffalo Bill's Wild West Show embellished many a store front

Annie was a master shot with all firearms—rifle, shotgun and pistol. She was a world champion with the shotgun, beating all comers, including the Grand Duke Michael of Russia. One of her favorite tricks, which she performed regularly in Buffalo Bill's Wild West Show, was to ride full speed around the arena shooting glass balls that her husband threw into the air for her. As a special feat, Frank would throw six balls into the air at once, and Annie would break them all before they hit the ground. But her most famous trick of all was to puncture with six shots, before it hit the ground, a playing card that Frank threw into the air.

Annie Oakley was probably the best known trick shooter ever associated with Remington guns, but she was by no means the only one.

Annie Oakley, famous markswoman

Buffalo Bill Cody, shown during a tour of Europe

Another very famous shot was the Italian General Pisano. His favorite firearm was the model 24 autoloader, a .22 caliber rifle that first came out in 1922. Its magazine would hold fifteen .22 shorts or ten long rifle cartridges, and General Pisano made the most of this capacity. One of his most spectacular tricks was to play a tune on an organ by shooting at the keys.

The .22 caliber autoloaders were primarily for marksmen and hunters of small game. But there were high powered autoloaders, too. The original model 8 had been made in .30, .32 and .35 caliber as well as .25. In 1936, the first of the famous "Woodsmaster" autoloaders appeared. Later models offered even more powerful loads, and the series still continues today.

Small game or big game, trick shooting or plinking, the successors of John Browning's original models still provide sport for American shooters. The reputation for fine workmanship and fair dealing that had brought John and Matthew to Marcellus Hartley's door had paid off very well indeed.

One of the many awards captured by Annie Oakley

123

CHAPTER NINE

THE CASE OF THE CLEAN BORE

The trouble with guns was that you
were everlastingly cleaning them—
until James Burns had a brainstorm

THE CASE OF THE CLEAN BORE

Autoloader or muzzle-loader, rifle, shotgun or pistol, all guns had one annoying drawback in common. Their bores had to be cleaned thoroughly after each use. Some especially fastidious shooters even went to the extreme of cleaning them out after each shot. The American marksmen in the Creedmoor matches had done this, for example. It made for a long afternoon, and it really wasn't necessary, but these gun lovers were so thoroughly aware of the ruin that could be caused by leaving a barrel uncleaned after a day's shooting that they were taking no chances in such an important match.

It had always been so. The earliest gunpowder was made of charcoal, sulphur and saltpeter. When it burned, it left a gummy residue in the bore, called fouling. After a number of shots, the barrel would get so full of this fouling that it would be difficult to get the bullet in. If the fouling was not cleaned out when the shooter finished with the day's shooting, it would ruin the bore. For one thing, it attracted water that caused rust; for another, this water mixed with the sulphur residue and formed sulphuric acid, which also ate holes in the iron. The only way to get rid of the fouling was to pour water, preferably hot water, through the bore until it dissolved the residue, then wipe it dry and oil it well.

Preceding page: Remington center fire rifle, center fire pistol and revolver, and rim fire cartridges, and shotgun shells—fastest, 4100 feet per second.

THE CASE OF THE CLEAN BORE

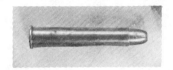

A breakthrough came in the last years of the nineteenth century. Smokeless powder became practical for both sporting and military cartridges. It quickly became popular. This new powder, based on nitrocellulose particles, burned cleanly and completely. It left absolutely no harmful deposit in the gun barrels through which it passed.

This was a happy situation indeed, but unfortunately the shooter could not yet throw away his cleaning kit. All guns now fired self-contained metallic cartridges, and these cartridges contained an explosive primer to set off the powder charge. Even if the powder was harmless, the primer was highly destructive. All primers then in use contained potassium chlorate. When mixtures containing chlorate exploded, they released a very corrosive gas that lingered in the bore, where its residue produced quick corrosion if not promptly removed. The only way to get rid of this residue was to use the same sort of treatment that had been standard for the black powder fouling.

James E. Burns, inventor of non-corrosive primer

Remington designers and the Remington management were well aware of the desirability of a non-corrosive primer, but the question was how to make it.

As it often does, opportunity arrived when it was least expected. This time it came, on a cold winter day in 1924, in the form of a chemist named James E. Burns, who had recently left the employ of the United States Cartridge Company. Burns was on his way to Florida to seek some warmer weather, but before leaving

Remington shotgun shells, such as the "Express," come encased in plastic, affording greater stability and reliable chambering

he stopped in to pay a call on Egbert C. Hadley and W. E. Witsil, of Remington's technical staff. The three were old friends, and neither Hadley nor Witsil was too alarmed when Burns pulled out a revolver and proceeded to fire six quick shots in the office. After all, he was a well known "character." They were a bit relieved, however, to note that the loads were blanks. When he had finished his fusillade, Burns looked up at the people who had come running from all over the building, handed the revolver to Hadley and asked him to put it away in a good damp place until he returned from Florida in a month or so. Without even wiping the gun out, Hadley complied.

After his trip to the South, Burns returned as he had promised and asked to see his pistol. Hadley had found a damp place all right, and even the blued exterior of the gun had started to show signs of rust. Burns, however, was interested only in the interior. He ran a rag through the bore and the chambers and

128

Loading the Remington M/58 automatic shotgun; as many as 3 shells can be loaded in seconds

Shotgun shell; center fire rifle, and .22 rim fire cartridges

squinted through them at the light. Without a word he handed the gun over to Hadley and Witsil, who did the same. To their amazement, the bore was as clean and bright as the day it was made. Burns had invented a non-corrosive primer! Seldom were two men so excited. Here was the answer to every shooter's dream. Remington hired Burns almost on the spot, so they could be the first to offer the boon to the hunters and marksmen of the nation.

It is often a long step from invention to production, however. Burns' primers had been made by hand in a small quantity, and they had not had to endure the long shelf life, under varied storage conditions, that a successful commercial cartridge would have to undergo. More tests and more experimentation were necessary. Remington chemists immediately went to work on the project. They finally produced a commercially feasible primer, using lead styphnate. The only drawback to this was the fact that the material

129

was produced commercially only in Europe, though Du Pont was working on it experimentally in this country. Remington could not wait for someone else. They sent their own men to Europe, bought foreign patents, and brought back technicians to set up a plant to manufacture lead styphnate at Remington. In about two years, they were ready to produce new non-corrosive cartridges for the American sportsmen.

The tests that preceded this great event, however, were almost unbelievable in their variety and intensity. Millions of rounds were fired, some in Remington laboratories, some in shooting galleries in New York City with which the Company had made special testing arrangements. Some of the guns used were left uncleaned and almost untouched for eighteen months. Others were put in a laboratory wet chamber, where the relative humidity reached 90 per cent at a temperature of 120°. Still other guns were placed in the annealing rooms, where clouds of steam created a veritable Turkish bath. Exteriors rusted under these conditions, but the bores remained bright as mirrors. Not only did the new primers fail to release a harmful residue, they even spread a protective coating on the bore! Here was a real bonus that Remington chemists had not even anticipated when they began their work. The more often a sportsman fired his gun, the better he protected it against rust. The breakthrough had become a revolution.

By 1926, the new non-corrosive cartridges

Remington center fire rifle, revolver and pistol cartridges; bullet styles range from full patch to pointed soft point

were ready for release, but they still had no name. As a promotion measure as well as an attempt to get a suitable designation for the new ammunition, Remington held a contest to choose the name. Two men, a thousand miles apart, came up with the final answer— "Kleanbore." Maybe it was obvious. Certainly it fitted. Both men received prizes, and the new cartridges quickly found their way to the shelves of all sporting goods stores, where they were snapped up by shooters in every part of the country. Once the breakthrough had been made, other cartridge companies were quick to follow suit. All of them now offer non-corrosive ammunition. But once again Remington had been first.

131

CHAPTER TEN

THE REMINGTONS THAT WENT TO WAR

World War I's big production hazard was the Czar's inspector, explosive in more ways than one

Sporting arms have always been the principal interest, indeed the lifeblood, of Remington. But the company has been willing to undertake the production of military weapons whenever it seemed in the national interest.

One of the first arms that appealed to Remington designers as a possible successor to the rolling block was the Keene repeater. During the 1870's, John W. Keene of Newark, New Jersey, had patented a number of improvements that he finally assembled into a bolt action arm with a tubular magazine under the barrel. It was an unusual bolt action, in that there was an outside hammer. When the shooter pulled the bolt up and back, then shoved it forward and down in the usual fashion, it ejected the empty cartridge case if there was one in the chamber and fed a fresh round into position. The hammer, however, still had to be cocked separately, by hand. A magazine cut-off on the left side of the receiver permitted the arm to be used as a single-loader, with a full magazine in reserve if the shooter so desired. This was considered an important factor by most firearms authorities at that time. Magazine capacities varied from seven to nine shots, depending on whether the piece was carbine or full rifle length. The Remington people liked the Keene well enough to buy the rights to it and to manufacture sporting

Remington guns for the war. Starting on the left and going clockwise: model A-3 Springfield, the Enfield model 17 and the A3-03, a product of 1941

rifles in several grades. They also thought the arm had military potential, and so they offered it to the government. But the Army still preferred the single-shot trapdoor Springfield, and the Navy had little need for small arms. A few carbines and rifles were purchased in 1880, but hardly enough to count.

At almost the same time, however, Remington had found an infinitely better rifle, and the company quickly shifted its attention to it. This time the inventor was James Paris Lee, a native Scot who had become a naturalized citizen. He was also one of the world's foremost gun designers. His new rifle featured a revolutionary box magazine mounted right under the action. It would hold five cartridges, which were pushed directly up into the receiver by a small sturdy spring. It was simpler, cheaper and stronger than the common tubular magazines of the period, and it was less susceptible to injury than most of the versions then on the market. It also made use of the bolt action, but this time the movement of the bolt also cocked the hammer. Here was a gun design that seemed ideal for both civilian and military use, and Remington jumped at the opportunity to manufacture it.

The Lee was a successful arm in both departments. Bolt action sporting arms with the new box magazine were quickly recognized as fine guns and the Navy also bought some military versions of the rifle in 1881 and 1882. Unfortunately, this was just at the time when the Remington Company found itself in dire

Remington-Keene repeater, with a tubular magazine

Above: model 51 automatic. Left, top: Mark III signal pistol. Left, below: Parker 35mm. signal pistol Mark I

financial straits, after the death of Sam Remington in 1882. When the firm went into recievership a couple of years later, it lost the rights to Lee's design, so that it could not develop the fine arm still further. It was an ironic quirk of fate that these events took place just as they did, for a very short time after Remington lost its rights to the Lee system, the British Government adopted it as part of their famous Lee-Enfield rifle. Had the company been able to hold out a little longer, its financial worries might have been over sooner.

In the summer of 1914, France asked the Remington company to make a few thousand of its old standard Lebel rifles, a bolt-action arm it had first adopted in 1886. This put no strain on the facilities in Ilion. But then came the British, and their needs were great. They wanted a million Enfield rifles as soon as possible, and then perhaps another million after that. What was more, they wanted these Enfields to be redesigned to fire the new .303 cartridge. Remington was asked to do the redesigning, make the necessary machinery, gauges and tools, and start delivery of finishèd rifles in less than a year and a half.

This was a tremendous task, but Remington

Russian troops at inspection. They are carrying Remington-made Mosin-Nagants of which the Czarist government ordered a million

did not hesitate. The nation might be officially neutral, but there was no question about personal sentiments. Marcellus Hartley Dodge signed the contract with the British in October, 1914. Then he set out to borrow the necessary money to build new factories. There just wasn't enough room in the old plant at Ilion. He erected a new one next to it, then leased and remodeled a half-finished locomotive factory in Pennsylvania, which became known as the Eddystone Arsenal. Working almost around the clock, Remington engineers designed new machines and tools, supervised their construction and installation in the brand new assembly lines. In a phenomenal feat, the first Remington-made Enfield rifles were tested at Ilion in October, 1915, just a year after the signing of the contract and well before the January 1, 1916, deadline, when actual deliveries had to be made. In a few

137

American soldiers with the United States model 1917, a caliber .30

more months, the new factories reached their production goal of 2,000 or more finished rifles a day—all of them manufactured to exacting standards.

No sooner had the British contract come under control than another of the allies came to Remington asking for arms to help fight the enemy. This time it was Russia, and the Czar's government also wanted a million rifles. These were to be Mosin-Nagants, a bolt-action magazine weapon developed back in 1891 and firing the 7.62 mm. Russian cartridge. Remington agreed to make them, and signed a contract in **138** 1915. Again a new factory was needed, and this

version of the Enfield bolt-action box magazine repeating rifle

one was built in Bridgeport, the home of the Union Metallic Cartridge Company half of the Remington operation.

If the British contract production had gone smoothly, the Russian contract was the exact opposite. The official blueprints, master models and gauges all differed from one another. Inspectors and fitters went mad trying to put parts together and test them. Every rifle had to be fitted by hand, with time-consuming filing and shaving. Instead of 2,000 arms a day, the Bridgeport plant was turning out 125. It was failing to meet its agreed deliveries and it was losing a great deal of money in the process. **139**

The first Browning machine gun ever produced by Remington. The gun was a mainstay of WW I

This was an impossible situation. Remington engineers reworked the official Russian standards and finally obtained official approval from the Czar's representatives.

This cleared up the technical difficulties, but there were still other hurdles—fifteen hundred of them, in fact. These were the host of official inspectors sent by the Russian government to make sure that the rifles were made according to specifications. Each one inspected as if his life depended upon it. They got in each other's way and, more important, they got in the workmen's way and so succeeded in delaying the production.

It was a trying situation for the Remington gunsmiths, and company tradition still fondly recalls the comeuppance meted out to one of the most obnoxious of the Czar's minions. This one was a Cossack captain, who appeared at the plant each day attired in full regalia, with fur hat, flowing coat, red leather boots, crossed bandoliers and a gold-sheathed dagger.

Shells of all kinds were in demand for the war effort. These were produced in Bridgeport, Conn.

He was so spectacular that the men promptly dubbed him "Alexander the Great." In time, the workmen got to accept the fancy costume, but they mightily resented his particular specialty in inspecting arms. Alexander had a dread fear of accidental rifle discharges caused by jars or shocks. To make sure that the Remington-made Mosin-Nagants were safe from this hazard, he would seize finished arms, load and cock them, then slam their butts on the concrete floor with all his might. He never did succeed in getting a rifle to fire accidentally, but he broke an awful lot of stocks trying.

Human endurance can stretch just so far. Finally the Remington gunsmiths decided they had had enough, and that Alexander should be taught a lesson. They took a newly finished rifle and filed the sear nose so that it barely held the hammer cocked. True to form, Alexander loaded and cocked the piece, poised it and slammed it to the floor. The rifle went off with a bang magnified hundreds of times by

Remington's Ammunition Works in Brimsdown, Middlesex, Eng.

141

The Browning machine gun, although heavy to carry, was a hard gun to get past once entrenched in a fox hole or other bunker

the reverberations inside the building. The bullet whistled up past Alexander's face—and punctured a 4-inch high-pressure water pipe directly above his head! As Alexander instinctively glanced up after the bullet, he caught the full force of the gushing water in his face. It is doubtful that a 7.62 mm. hole could have done more than douse his enthusiasm, but stories grow with the telling, especially good stories. And at Remington one hears the Russian was knocked off his feet and that laughing workmen had to drag him to safety to keep him from being drowned!

Despite technical and human difficulties, Remington eventually got the Russian contract under control.

In 1917, America needed arms of its own. Production of the fine 1903 Springfield was well underway, but it was dreadfully slow. If an army was to be sent to Europe to help the embattled Allies, the United States had to

An ingenious and powerful device was the Army's grenade-throwing rifle, used in both World Wars

obtain rifles quickly. Remington still had the machinery for making the British Enfield. It offered to rechamber this model to fire the Springfield .30-06 cartridge, and Ordnance quickly accepted, designating the rifle the model 1917. Within weeks, Remington was ready for production and by December it could produce better than 3,000 of the new models a day. In all, Remington made 545,541 model 1917 Enfields at Ilion and 1,181,908 at the Eddystone Arsenal. One million of them were still stored in government arsenals at the end of the war. Even though too late for World War I, these fine rifles were not wasted. After Dunkirk, they were sent to England to help save that nation from the threatened German invasion of 1940. In addition, the Russian rifle plant at Bridgeport was converted to make Browning heavy machine guns, automatic rifles, automatic pistols and signal pistols.

When all was said and done, it was a re- **143**

One of America's most effective war guns was the Thompson submachine gun, for which Remington made barrels and other parts

markable record. Remington had manufactured a large percentage of all the rifles made for American forces during the war.

Twenty years after the first one, America was again at war, and the Springfields rolling off the Remington line were vitally needed for national defense. They were vastly different Springfields from the original 1903 model. When Remington first began making them for the British, they found that the government model was almost a bench-made firearm, requiring a great amount of handwork. It could not be made practically as a commercial venture. Immediately they set about redesigning it and produced the famous model A3-03, carried by many an American soldier in World

War II. The standard model 1903 Springfield had 91 parts. Remington promptly eliminated 12 of them. Other parts, which had required forging or hand work, were redesigned so they could be stamped. Only 24 parts remained unchanged! The resulting gun was just as good as the original. It was just as sturdy, and it shot just as straight. But it was lighter, it was less expensive and, above all, it was much faster to make. In all wartime endeavors, time is of first importance, and the Remington redesign was of tremendous help in making sure that American troops were rapidly and fully armed.

In addition to their outstanding success with the model A3, Remington also designed the model A4, an especially accurate rifle for snipers, and they made shotguns and .22 rifles for training purposes, plus barrels and other parts for the Thompson sub-machine gun.

The company's contributions to national defense in both World Wars were by no means limited to firearms, however. In World War I, the company produced over 50 per cent of the small arms ammunition made in this country for the United States and her allies. In World War II, Remington operated its own ammunition plants at peak capacity and, in addition, designed, built, and operated five government-owned ammunition factories.

Remington's contributions, in both of these conflicts, represented quite a record for a firm whose main interests and personal profit opportunities lay in the field of sporting firearms and ammunition.

145

CHAPTER ELEVEN

"TOO FAST TO BE SEEN WITH THE NAKED EYE"

With the coming of peace, the way was clear for new designs, new concepts, new "families of guns"

"TOO FAST TO BE SEEN WITH THE NAKED EYE"

There have been many dramatic improvements in the manufacture of American sporting firearms and ammunition in the days since the founding of Remington Arms in 1816. From the crude muzzle loaders of the early 1800's to the precision rifles and shotguns of today, these changes have reflected the ever-improving technology of an industry that has geared itself to meet the needs of America's sportsmen.

As a result of all the advances made in the last one hundred and fifty years, in a field in which improvements had been relatively slow for several previous centuries, it seemed to many people that the development of sporting firearms and ammunition had reached its zenith by the late 1930's.

In 1933, E. I. Du Pont de Nemours and Company purchased a 60 per cent interest in Remington. The infusion of new blood from this great organization resulted in a number of new ideas that had just begun to reach fruition when World War II began. As we have already seen, Remington devoted all of its facilities to military production during the war, but with the return of peace, efforts were again turned to new concepts in the design and manufacture of sporting firearms and ammunition. As a result of Remington's leadership, the years since 1945 have been witness to even

 Preceding page: model 700 ADL big game rifle, model 660 carbine, model 760 "Gamemaster" pump action big game rifle, model 742 "Woodsmaster" automatic big game rifle

more startling improvements. These improvements have included a parade of new models, new calibers and new production concepts that, taken in the whole, represent a major breakthrough in firearms manufacture.

Starting with the earliest of its post-war models in 1948, Remington has gone on to design and produce a complete new "family of guns" that has captured the imagination of the shooting public. Included in the all-new Remington line today are three bolt action center fire rifles, a gas-operated autoloading shotgun, an autoloading shotgun, a pump action shotgun, a slide action high power rifle, a gas-operated autoloading high power rifle, three autoloading .22 caliber rim fire rifles, a slide action .22 caliber rim fire rifle, three bolt action rim fire rifles, and a bolt action target rifle (available in rim or center fire versions) .

The Du Pont Company's founder Eleuthère Irénée du Pont de Nemours

Before actual designing of these new guns was started, Remington interviewed thousands of shooters to find out what they wanted in the way of new models. As a result of this survey, the company had a firm foundation on which to build plans for the future.

In designing new models to meet the needs found in this and subsequent surveys, some entirely new concepts in manufacturing have been used. For example, the demand for lighter weight guns in combination with heavier loads necessitated a search for new materials and new methods for containing the higher impact stresses. As a result, in shotguns

149

Remington—then and 1947. Left to right: Eliphalet Remington, Franklin Remington, Marcellus Hartley Dodge, Marcellus Hartley

the actions were redesigned so that breech bolts could be locked up more securely, using a barrel extension made of tougher high strength steels. The closer tolerances possible also opened the door for barrel interchangeability, eliminated the need for hand fitting should a shooter decide to make a replacement with a different type of barrel.

In Remington's models 700 and 660 bolt action center fire, high power rifles, the bolt heads were redesigned to provide a hardened steel shroud and thus give greater support to the base of the cartridge, with resulting greater strength and safety. This was made possible through the design of a novel "wrap-around" extractor of spring steel, which fits snugly in a circular groove enclosed within the bolt shroud.

One of the most interesting breakthroughs in materials for firearms was signaled by the Remington "Nylon 66" autoloading .22 cal-

150

Remington's 10,000,000th sporting gun, a model 11-48 shotgun given to Marcellus Hartley Dodge

Presentation plaque of the 10,000,000th Remington Arms gun

iber rifle. Made of a combination of structural nylon and ordnance steel, this little rifle has set new standards of performance. Because the nylon stock and fore-end do not warp or change dimensions, barrel bedding is extremely uniform, improving accuracy. The stock is extremely strong, and because all moving parts bear on nylon, lubrication is unnecessary. The result is a gun that has won universal acclaim from shooters for its light weight, ease of handling, accuracy and ruggedness.

A very important phase of designing that has contributed to the major breakthrough for Remington is the development of a high degree of interchangeability of parts. This has enabled the company to produce so-called "families of guns"—guns of the shotgun type, guns of the high power rifle type, and guns of the low power (or .22 caliber) class, all with a similar look and "feel." Throughout these gun

151

Top to bottom: model 40X target rifle, model 700 custom bolt action center fire rifle, model 700 ADL bolt action center fire rifle, model 788 bolt action big game rifle

types, the parts can be replaced, with no factory fitting, in guns of the same model or class, thus making repairs much easier.

Continued study of new processes and material has enabled Remington to produce guns of lighter and more compact design. Increased use of new welding techniques, lighter metal, explorations and research into the very nature of metal itself, have revealed new ways of forming gun parts. Appearance and durability of stocks and fore-ends have been vastly improved by use of a new Du Pont developed wood finish known as RK-W.

Another angle of modern gun designing that has played an important part in quality built

Left to right: model 870 "Wingmaster" pump action shotgun, model 1100 automatic shotgun, model 552BDL .22 automatic rifle, model 572BDL .22 pump action rifle

into every Remington gun is the use of high speed photography. To produce a gun that will perform as designed requires continuous study and testing of the pilot models. The reaction of the critical area of design, particularly in autoloading shotguns, is too fast to evaluate with the naked eye. A cutaway model is made, loaded and fired under the critical scrutiny of a high speed camera. The action can then be slowed, studied, and, if necessary, traced on actual charts for evaluation.

The innovations which have characterized Remington's improvements in firearms designs have had their counterpart in the ammunition field. In the last twenty years, the com-

153

Model 29, 12-gauge slide (pump) action repeating shotgun

pany has introduced a host of new center fire cartridges, ranging from flat shooting varmint calibers such as the 222 Remington, 222 Remington Magnum, 223 Remington and 22-250 Remington; through medium sized big game loads, such as the 6 mm. Remington and 280 Remington; to belted magnum cartridges, such as the 7 mm. Remington Magnum and the 350 Remington Magnum. The company started a revolution in shotgun shell design with the introduction of its plastic loads in 1960. Completely scuff and mar proof and impervious to the effects of weather, these shells will chamber in guns under all conditions. Further improved with the introduction of a new plastic wad column in 1963, which gives improved patterns and reduces recoil, they have obsoleted the old paper and brass shells, and other manufacturers are now following Remington's lead.

Any study of modern gun and ammunition manufacture would be incomplete, and any story of a breakthrough to higher ground in the art of production and design of these products would be worthless, if Remington's more than 150 years of experience were not considered. The combination of father-to-son tradition, coupled with modern research methods and advanced development, creates a certain pride of accomplishment. Such a combination of heritage and talent has been the key to Remington's success in presenting to the shooting public the finest products of the gunmakers' skill.

From top to bottom: model 591 5mm. Remington rim fire magnum, nylon 66 .22 automatic rim fire rifle, nylon 77 .22 clip automatic, model 581 left hand bolt action .22 rim fire rifle

INDEX